TO - MA.

FROM - OLIVE + PETE

W9-BFH-511

CONFESSIONS
of a HAPPY MAN

By <u>ART</u> <u>LINKLETTER</u>

PEOPLE ARE FUNNY

KIDS SAY THE DARNDEST THINGS

THE SECRET WORLD OF KIDS

CONFESSIONS OF A HAPPY MAN

CONFESSIONS
of a HAPPY MAN

BY *Art Linkletter*

with Dean Jennings

Published by <u>BERNARD</u> <u>GEIS</u> <u>ASSOCIATES</u>

Distributed by Random House

Library of Congress Catalog Card Number: 60-16866

Manufactured in the United States of America
by American Book–Stratford Press, New York

SECOND PRINTING

To Lois

Contents

CONFESSIONS
of a HAPPY MAN

1. Kelly Is the Name

SOMEWHERE IN CANADA—and the name of the city must remain my secret—a very special couple may be turning on their television set today to watch my show.

I wish I could see their faces when the announcer calls out my name. It is a name they know very well. Many times I imagine the subtle exchange of glances between the man and the woman, a look that is probably a mixture of pride and guilt. If there are visitors in their living room, they cannot talk intimately about me. They can never say what they really think, for I am a name and a person out of their past, and it is a past they have obviously tried to forget.

The name of this couple is Kelly, and this is the only clue I can give.

Mr. and Mrs. Kelly of Canada.

They are my real parents, and I am their son, Gordon Arthur Kelly, better known in show business as Art Linkletter. I have never met them, nor have I had any contact with them since they deserted me forty-eight years ago, when I was only a few weeks old. The Kellys have two other sons and a daughter—my brothers and sisters, of course—and I have not met them nor heard from them either. I never really expected a friendly word from my parents. I would be surprised and disconcerted if there was such word, because I am their nagging conscience. I am the child they put out of their lives far from home.

In the life of every man and woman there are undoubtedly many little knifing secrets they have often wanted to bring out into the light. The true story of my real parentage has been my personal secret for years, and I am talking about it now because my experience may be of some comfort to an adopted child, and I was one, or to some young couple caught in a tragic dilemma, which, for one reason or another, forces them to run away and hide until it's over.

It occurs to me, as I start my book, that this may be a surprisingly serious vein for an entertainer who, to the public at least, is considered a gay, happy man without a solemn thought in his head.

"Harlequin without his mask," Thackeray once wrote, "is known to present a very sober countenance." In my story I want to avoid this sort of Jekyll-Hyde suggestion because I do not really have a dual personality. The Linkletter you see on your TV screen is the same Linkletter who kids around at home with his children and grandchildren. In fact, I am unrestrained in either place, and I had thought of beginning this story with an experience I had at Las Vegas one day last winter when my wife, Lois, and I were lolling around a swimming pool there.

The place was quite a sight. The shimmering blue water, with no one in it. The beautiful show girls in their cleaving Bikinis. The handsome young men reading the *Racing Form* and figuring the odds on horses and girls alike. Anyway, there was this stunning brunette on the far side of the pool, and she couldn't take her eyes off me. "You see, dear," I whispered to Lois, "I have fascinated this girl. After all these years the fatal Linkletter charm still works."

"Really?" Lois said.

"Yes. Look, here she comes for a two-point landing."

The doll glided clear around the pool and came right up to me with her big violet eyes putting out about a thousand watts.

"Oh . . . Mr. Linkletter . . ." she said.

"Yes?" I responded eagerly.

"I sat on your lap on television once."

"You *did?*"

"Yes, sir," she said. "When I was five years old."

I was suddenly an elderly gentleman of forty-eight. I dove to the bottom of the pool, and I wouldn't have come up at all except that it was lunchtime. Not long afterward, I was named Grandfather of the Year, and I accepted the award at an impressive ceremony at the Waldorf in New York. "What did you get?" Lois asked when I called her at home that evening, "a set of crutches or a wheel chair?" It occurred to me then that it is later than I think, and that I'd better tell my story while there is still time. And the Las Vegas incident, I thought, was in character with the Linkletter the public knows.

But there is also a Linkletter no one knows.

ii

My life began in the little city of Moose Jaw, in the Canadian province of Saskatchewan, on July 17, 1912. Moose Jaw is 375 miles west of Winnipeg, on the Moose Jaw River, and was so named because it was a place where, according to the historians, "white man mended his cart with the jaw of a moose."

The only moose remaining there now, I suppose, are those who go to the lodge hall. I don't really know, because I have never been back. Many of the good people there write to me, the newspaper refers to me as a local boy, and I have been named an honorary citizen of the town. I have often thought that a return visit to my birthplace might help mend my mental cart, but I am almost afraid to face the inevitable disillusionment of reality. It will not be as I have dreamed it to be.

I have never known whether I was born in a hospital or a private home, and I don't know the name of the doctor who delivered me. I have never even seen a picture of my parents, and the records of the Children's Aid Society, a Canadian government agency, show only that a child named Gordon Arthur Kelly was born in Moose Jaw that July day in 1912.

As I thumb over my many scrapbooks, letters, program scripts and other souvenirs of my twenty-six years in show business, I am struck with the curious and perhaps significant fact that there has been a dominant theme in my interviews with adults and children. Two questions I have asked over and over, for instance, are: "Where were you born?" and "How did your parents meet?" and I have had some quite remarkable replies.

On one show I have never forgotten, my guest was Mrs. Lillian Fontaine of Saratoga, California—the charming mother of two great movie stars, Olivia de Havilland and Joan Fontaine.

"Where were your beautiful daughters born?" I asked.

"In Tokyo," she said.

"In Tokyo!" I exclaimed. "How on earth did *that* happen?"

"Oh . . ." she said lamely, "in the regular way."

Then just last spring, I was chatting with a pretty little seven-year-old girl on my House Party show, and I asked her how her parents met. "Oh," she said, "they didn't meet."

"But they had to meet somewhere," I said.

"Well," she said, "they were roommates in college."

If the tables were turned and some interviewer asked me

these same questions, I wouldn't have any clear answers at all. I only know that my father was a high school teacher who brought his sweetheart to Moose Jaw, where they were not known, and that they went back to their hometown in another part of Canada immediately after I was born. They left me with the Children's Aid Society where, for a time at least, I was also registered under my mother's maiden name.

Last summer I had a letter from a woman in Texas, a very poignant note in which she said she was expecting another baby. Her husband was unemployed, they were completely without funds, and the expected baby was a burden they couldn't handle. "We know you love children," she wrote, "and our child would have a far better life with you. We want to give you this baby with no strings attached."

I told her, as gently as I could, to stick it out and keep the child. I told her that inevitably the child would learn that he or she was an unwanted baby, and would never forgive them. These wounds never heal. I know.

I do not intend to sit in judgment on my parents, nor to question their right to reject me. I suppose there are circumstances when terrible decisions must be made because there is no choice, but there are no clues when you walk in the dark as I have done all my life. Perhaps my father would have lost his job if anyone had known why he had to leave home so suddenly and mysteriously. Perhaps he was broke at the time. Perhaps neither of them was ready for marriage and parenthood. I'm sure it doesn't matter now. It is a painful subject to me, especially because I have never quite stifled the resentment I felt when I accidentally discovered that the Kellys had put me out for adoption, only to go home and be married and have other children they obviously wanted to keep.

Thirty years ago, when I was eighteen and first had the urge to travel, I wrote to the Children's Aid Society:

"I intend to travel," I said, "and for that reason I am writing to you. It will be necessary for me to have my birth certificate in order to get a passport. As my (foster) parents are not sure where it is, I am writing to you and taking the liberty of asking you to get it for me. Also, if possible, I should like a little information about my real parents' position and occupations. Of course, it is only natural that I should like to know something of my parents in order that I may better know my own capabilities."

I got the birth certificate, but nothing else. Either the Society didn't have the information, or they were unwilling to give it to me. I waited another thirteen years before I learned my father's name and where he lived.

With the passing of the years, my curiosity about my parents has been dulled to the point where I no longer care. But every man has moments when, no matter how much he is loved or surrounded by love, he is lonely and agonizingly alone. And during those moments, when the world and people and my own loved ones seemed to be as distant as a desert mirage, I thought often about Mr. and Mrs. Kelly of Canada. I imagined myself driving down an elm-shaded street to a small brown house with a front porch, and walking up to the door and touching the bell with a shaking finger. And they would open the door and their arms would be around me, and they would whisper: "Son, welcome home, son."

But in my heart I knew it would never happen, and it never has. Indeed, as time went on, my curiosity was distorted by rancor, as though there were a chip on my shoulder and I was taunting them to knock it off. *I don't need you any more*, I told myself. *I've made out all right. You go your way and I'll go mine.* I have never been able to silence this inner voice of mine, and I wonder if I ever can.

iii

There were a number of couples who wanted to adopt children from the Society office in Moose Jaw and among them were two people, John and Mary Linkletter, who, it seems to me, would have been the last to qualify as prospective parents. John Linkletter was then fifty-one years old, a tall, heavy man with thick graying hair who was a familiar figure on the streets of Moose Jaw because he walked with a marked limp. His right leg had been amputated after a boyhood accident, and he walked on a wooden leg with the support of a stout cane. There was a stiff metal hinge where his knee should have been, and with each step he had to give a little kick to snap the hinge into position.

Much later, when I learned to know him better, I noticed that he often used this snapping motion to emphasize his words, and he would impale the air with his cane as though it were an exclamation point.

He not only refused to complain about his leg (and it pained him often when the weather was cool or damp) but he was fond of quoting a line attributed to the late author, Albert Edward Wiggam: "Wooden legs are not inherited, but wooden heads are." Needless to say, I have since been deeply concerned with the problems of the physically handicapped and have made countless fund-raising appearances for these groups. Once in a while I have had heart-warming rewards, such as the letter from a woman in New Jersey, telling me that she desperately needed a new wooden leg. "If you could help me out," she said, "I will promise to print your name and broadcast-times on the new leg, and I'll wear transparent stockings so everybody can see it. That will give you lots of publicity because I go everywhere."

No one could ignore this blithe spirit. I told her I could get along without the publicity, but that she couldn't get along without her leg. I sent her the money, remembering a determined old man who hobbled around all his life with not a glum word about his trouble.

John Linkletter was an insurance salesman when he and his wife, Mary, a plump, round-faced little woman, adopted me in Moose Jaw. I never asked either of them why they chose to adopt a child so late in life, but they had lost a baby years before and were not able to have another, and were undoubtedly lonely. The Linkletters were both from Prince Edward Island —there are distant relatives still living there—and, like other pioneers, they had come to western Canada and its challenging new frontier. The name Linkletter, or so the authorities say, comes from an old Norse word Lingklettar, meaning large stones. In Scotland, the equivalent word was Heathercletts, meaning big rocks conspicuous in the heather.

In any case, it is certainly an unusual name, and I am naturally proud that I have helped to make it well known. I recall one press agent who, when I was starting out, said dolefully: "With a name like Linkletter you'll never be big. It's too long for the headlines. Now if you could change it to something short like Hope, Crosby, Berle or Cantor, you'd have it made." I was tempted to tell him I was born with the name Kelly, and I am sure he would have yelled: "Great! Art Kelly! It's a natural."

I don't know whether I "have it made" by press agent standards, but it is rewarding when other Linkletters around the country, including some Linklaters, Linkloters and others who say they are all in the same happy family, put the bite on me for a new car, a beach cottage, a trip to Hawaii or a

small loan of a thousand dollars, and so on. I particularly remember one Linkletter woman who begged for money on the
phone, saying she was my sister. My wife, Lois, took
the call and said: "I'm sorry, but Art doesn't have a sister
named Linkletter."

The woman was furious. "Well!" she snorted. "I never
thought Art would turn down his own flesh and blood." Lois
did not bother to explain, but had the woman talked to me I
might have told her that Linkletter not only means rocks in the
heather, but rocks in the head, thus not leaving much room for
anything else, including phony relatives.

My father and mother—as I will refer to them throughout
this story—were more rolling stones than rocks, and had moved
often during their early years together. I don't know why they
chose to live in Moose Jaw nor why, inexplicably, they suddenly abandoned the insurance business and took the long train
ride across the continent to set up housekeeping in Lowell,
Massachusetts.

There they opened a small variety store—a sort of neighborhood five-and-dime—and they were certain that this would be
the security for their later years. But my father had no business
sense at all, and the store was a dismal failure. At the end of
two years, bankrupt and disillusioned, they packed their bags
and migrated thirty-five hundred miles to a rickety little house
at Point Fermin, near San Pedro on the southern California
coast.

I have only shreds of memory about Point Fermin, but they
are indelible.

Once, climbing the cliffs a hundred feet above the sea, I
crawled out on a ledge to get a closer look at the plumes of
mist ricocheting from the rocks below. When I started back,
the crest was wet and slippery and pockmarked by the crashing
waves, and I was trapped. I clung to the hogback of the cliff

for hours until someone saw me there and heard my cries, and I was rescued with a fire department rope ladder.

The experience should have been a deterrent, but I have climbed many a cliff and mountain since, challenged by some emotion I cannot explain. The classic answer is that a man climbs a mountain because it's there, but I like the phrase coined by some unsung Hollywood gag man who said: "Mountain climbing is good because you never know when there'll be a tidal wave." I have even climbed the Matterhorn. At Disneyland, that is.

My other adventures in San Pedro were precipitated by an urgent need to earn spending money. In recent years, newspapermen and other unofficial biographers have occasionally referred to me as a millionaire. But I still pinch a penny now and then, and when I order dinner in a restaurant I instinctively glance at the price side of the menu. I can trace these habits back to my boyhood, when every spare dime looked like a little piece of Fort Knox. My foster parents, in their own way, gave me all the love and devotion any boy could expect, but I never had an allowance, and I was expected to pick up whatever I could with odd jobs.

The first money I ever earned came from a man with a small ice cream wagon. I was his shill.

On hot days, I wandered around licking double vanilla ice cream cones where other children could see me. I licked and slurped so enthusiastically that the man soon had kids standing in line in front of his truck. I still love ice cream and I still slurp. Somehow ice cream seems to taste better when you can wrap your tongue around it, but this is a habit frowned on by certain other members of my household.

Another time, when I was scrounging around the Point Fermin neighborhood for a dime or two, I met a pretty young housewife who wanted me to clean up her yard. She had a rockpile bigger than the one at San Quentin, and I spent one entire broiling Saturday afternoon hauling stones off the pile and arranging them in borders around her garden. When I finished, she said: "You're a nice little boy. What do you think I should pay you?"

Mother Linkletter had told me about Sir Galahad and how women rewarded him for his chivalry. And so I said: "Oh, that's all right, ma'am. I couldn't charge *you* anything."

"Well, now," she said. "That's very sweet of you. 'Bye."

She vanished inside the house, and left me standing there—with the blisters on my hands and my chin down to my knees, to say nothing of an empty pocket. I thought about this woman often as I began to get a name in radio and television. One day I was approached by an agent representing a promoter who wanted me to make a single appearance—what we call a one-nighter—in one of his theaters. This man had a reputation for exploiting struggling young entertainers, and cutting their fees to the barest minimum, but in this instance he needed me, and I knew he could pay.

"How much, Art?" the agent asked.

"Ten thousand," I said.

"Ten grand for a one-nighter?" he screamed. "What for?"

"For the rocks," I said.

I got it, too. And if the man reads this now, he will know exactly what I meant.

iv

I was probably six or seven years old when we left San Pedro and moved to East San Diego.

For a time, because Father couldn't afford to pay rent, we all lived in an old people's home maintained by one of the San

Diego churches. Father found a small vacant store and opened a shoe repair shop, a trade he had learned as a boy and had not practiced for many years. In time, because he was a skilled and conscientious workman, the cobbler shop began to prosper, and we were able to move to a house on Van Dyke Avenue.

As I look back on those early years, it seems to me that we were always living in little houses behind big houses, and as I grew older my one fervent wish was to have a street number without a ½ in it. The Van Dyke Avenue house was no exception. It was so ancient that it had an outhouse in the back yard, and more than once I have kiddingly told friends that the place had three rooms and a path. I mentioned it once to the late Producer Earl Carroll, and he said that under the circumstances I might enjoy seeing something ultra-modern. I dropped by his mansion one evening, and he hadn't exaggerated a bit. The faucets were gold, and the toilet seats were trimmed with mink.

Father Linkletter, who suddenly and dramatically got a call to serve the Lord just about the time I entered Central Grammar School in East San Diego, would have said such frills were the work of the Devil. He had always been intensely religious, but when the message came he turned preacher in the hellfire and damnation style. He could be violent on the subject of such human weaknesses as playing cards, smoking, movies and liquor.

Much later, when I was signed to emcee a show for the Roma Wine Company in 1939, I was afraid he would explode.

But to my surprise, he took the news with a philosophical shrug. "Well, Artie," he said, "Jesus turned water into wine. Also, if you know your Bible, you will remember the twenty-third verse of Timothy, Chapter V, which says: 'Drink no longer water, but use a little wine for thy stomach's sake and thine often infirmities.'"

"Thanks, Dad," I said. "I hope it will be a good show."

"All your shows are good," he said. "And when you can, Artie, give the Lord a little plug."

In the Twenties, the Rev. Mr. Linkletter—as he liked to be called, though he had no diploma and had never been ordained —was so busy plugging the Lord that his shoe repair business began to suffer. Every year, when spring came, he got restless and would hit the sawdust trail. He had no regular church of his own, preferring to fill in for vacationing ministers or, better yet, to gather a street corner crowd. I have vivid recollections of standing on hot dusty sidewalks in many a small town, beating a brass triangle to attract passers-by, and holding a collection plate.

My father was no Billy Sunday, but he had a voice like a big league umpire, and when he took on Satan no man could doubt his sincerity.

Unfortunately, there were always too few worshipers in these outdoor temples, and even those who heard him out contributed little or nothing to the plate I passed around. Yet even during these grim periods, my father said the Lord would provide (and indeed He did), and he used to tell my mother that with faith the merest shoestring could lead to good fortune.

Years later, when we started concocting unusual stunts for the People Are Funny show, I recalled my father's favorite thesis and decided to give it a test. From our audience we picked a war veteran who was unemployed and untalented, and who had exactly $18.25 to his name. We gave him a shoestring and nothing else, and told him to see what he could do with it.

He persuaded a woman in the audience to trade it for an old broken watch, and then conned a jeweler into fixing it for nothing. A week later, in our NBC studios, he raffled the repaired watch for seventy-five dollars. In six weeks, with our help, he had parlayed the shoestring into a new car, a share in an oil well, and a job as an auto salesman in Texas.

I eagerly reported this remarkable adventure to my father, and he nodded knowingly. "That man will bless you all his days," he said.

I don't know what kind of blessing Dad had in mind, but it had a most peculiar look when it finally came. The "lucky shoestring man," as we called him, sued me for $126,000, claiming we had promised him he would be rich for the rest of his life when he undertook the stunt. The oil well had not paid off, and, rather than being an ordinary car salesman, he thought he should have been made sales manager at the agency. I didn't have the heart to tell my father about this disillusioning aftermath—the case was settled for a few hundred dollars—but if I had, he surely would have said: "Turn the other cheek, Artie, and then you will be doubly blessed." Moreover, Dad would have brought him home for dinner.

He lived each day according to the teachings of the Bible, and he could not imagine that there were others who might disagree.

When customers came into his humble little cobbler shop, he not only fixed their shoes but he tried to repair their souls as well. He had a phenomenal knowledge of the Bible, could quote from it endlessly and accurately, and he always had just the right phrase for stubborn sinners. He often picked up straying lambs on the street and would persuade them to come to the house. These strangers were mostly bums or drunks or ex-cons, but I saw them as romantic adventurers from far-off worlds, and I learned more from them than I did from the other kids my age.

Our unwashed and unshaven guests were ushered into the house with old world courtliness, but before any food was served they had to sit still for a lengthy and flowery grace. Dad was never content to mumble empty phrases—as many a father does nowadays—and the ritual of grace to him was not only another Sermon on the Mount, but a complete roundup of the news.

If I had fallen off my borrowed bike and skinned a knee, he reported it in detail. If Mom was knitting a pair of socks or patching my torn and faded shirts, Dad would tell it with the breathless, exciting tone of a Winchell broadcast. If there were mice in the cellar—and there most certainly were—or if the roof was leaking, or some friend of the Lord had given us a jar of pickles, this was important news in every sense.

If the guest of the hour survived this long briefing—occasionally one of them would abruptly jump up and disappear through the door as though he had seen a cop—father would formally introduce him.

"Brother John Thompson is with us today, Lord," he would say. "He is a booze fighter and he has just finished a losing bout with Demon Rum. Today his head swims, his eyes burn, his tongue is dry, but tomorrow, with the Lord's help, he will be strong again." Or: "This is Brother Bill Bailey. He gambled his rent money on the horses, and has been evicted from his home. The Lord will teach him that some horses, like some people, do not run very fast."

More than likely, some of our raffish visitors were on the lam or could not be led from temptation even with the inducement of a large bowl of beef stew. I remember one of these characters whom Dad introduced as follows: "Dear Lord, Brother Eddie Smith is our friend for today. Eddie is a pickpocket, and with clever fingers he steals money from honest men's pockets."

When grace was finished, Brother Eddie was plainly indignant. "Who tole ya I was a wire?" he muttered.

"No one told me," my father said softly. "You pulled a dollar bill out of my pocket when you got here."

"I'm slippin'," Eddie said, red-faced. He fished the dollar from his pants pocket and silently handed it over.

"No, Brother Smith," my father said. "You need it more than I do. Consider it a gift from the Lord."

Later that evening, when Eddie had gone, Father was going through his pockets when he found two one-dollar bills. Brother Smith had picked his pocket again, in reverse, and had paid interest.

Watching these derelicts floating in and out of our little harbor, I saw—even as a boy—that they never left our house quite as lost as they were when they came. They might have drifted into the house with ill-concealed cynicism, or even with some hostility. They might have come just for the free meal, willing to take a little salvation talk in exchange for a plate of scrambled eggs. But when they left they had gained more than mere food. There was never a man so callous that he could not be softened by my father's generosity and his love for humanity, to say nothing of his faith and belief that there would be better days.

2. Lemons—5¢ a Dozen

There was an eight-year-old girl on my House Party show one afternoon, and I asked her: "What is your most secret wish?"

"I want to be ten years old all my life," she said.

"You don't want to grow up? Why?"

"Because," she said, "then I won't have to know about the birds and bees."

WHEN I WAS ten years old, the problem of the birds and the bees had not yet reared its interesting head.

The major dilemma in the Linkletter house always revolved around money and there never seemed to be any solution. We were incredibly poor, not only because Father was more pre-occupied with saving souls than facing the realities of life, but because he depended upon capricious fate to take care of our needs. I was wearing long pants, for instance—they were cut-downs donated by the Salvation Army—before I learned that not all families got their Thanksgiving and Christmas dinners in baskets.

Consequently, when other kids were playing sandlot ball after school or enjoying some other leisure activity, I was out hustling for those extra dimes and quarters that meant so much. I swept out stores. I was an errand boy. On weekends I went

27

from house to house in our neighborhood looking for odd jobs.

On one of these expeditions, I hitchhiked to Lemon Grove— a small town about five miles away—and discovered a number of lemon-packing plants. Behind one of them, crawling with insects, was a mound of what the trade calls culls, lemons which have been thrown out because they were rotten or were speckled with a sort of brown scale. The pile was about one hundred feet long and fifteen feet high, and in it were many lemons which had not yet fallen apart.

I took home a sackful, dumped them into an old galvanized tub my mother used for the family wash, and scrubbed off the brown spots with a stiff brush. I then hastily lugged them eight or ten blocks away—before they could spoil—and sold them to housewives for five cents a dozen. Within two weeks I had six other boys selling lemons for me—thus discovering the sound principle of having other people work for you—and I kept three cents out of each five-cent sale for myself.

It was a fine little business until one of my junior salesmen made the mistake of making a repeat call on one of his customers. The lady of the house met him at the door with a handful of stagnant lemons and angrily demanded her money back. Thereafter I tried to keep a record of streets we had already milked, but eventually we ran out of new territories, and the business folded up. To this day I can't pass the lemon bin in the supermarket without having my nose do a double twist, and when my children went through the lemonade-stand cycle, as many kids do, I was suddenly unavailable for advice.

The need for money could easily have turned me into a delinquent, and I don't know whether it was my father's training or just good luck that kept me out of trouble.

Some of my neighborhood pals stole regularly—tires, groceries, bicycles or anything within reach—but fortunately I was

never involved in any of these thefts. But there was one
period when three or four of us often jumped off San Diego
streetcars just as the conductor came through to collect the
fares. We got away with this for a month or two, and then one
day, with the conductor yelling cusses, we hit the pavement
alongside a passing car. The other boys scattered but I stood
there as the car stopped and a man's voice said: "Jump in, kid."
I scrambled into the car without hesitation and found myself
sitting with four uniformed cops.

"You beat 'em out of the fare, eh, kid?" one policeman said.

"Yes, sir," I said, "but I won't do it again."

"I'll say you won't," he said gruffly. "Because next time your
old man'll be hauled in to explain why his kid is a thief."

I was scared speechless. I could imagine my father's humiliation, to say nothing of his wrath, if his boy were brought into
court. The policeman could see that his warning had put me in
a panic, and he stopped the car. "Now you go home, boy," he
said. "But don't forget what I told you. It's kids like you who
wind up in the big house, and you wouldn't like it at all."

"I won't forget," I said devoutly. And I never did.

Long years later, Warden Clint Duffy invited me to entertain the inmates at San Quentin, and when the performance
ended in the huge mess hall, I was approached by a tall, sallow-
faced prisoner.

"Remember me, Art?" he said.

"I'm sorry," I said. "I've seen you somewhere, but—"

"The streetcar in San Diego," he said. "The day you jumped
off and got into a police car."

Suddenly I remembered. The scene took focus out of the
past, and now I knew the man's face. "Of course," I said. "Your
name is Bill, and you beat it down the street with the other kids
when I got in with the policemen."

"No, Art," he said. "I'm the cop who bawled you out."

ii

When I was about eleven years old, I was fortunate in getting a delivery route for a San Diego newspaper, the *Union*.

My district was the south side of University Avenue on the distant and shapeless boundary of East San Diego. It was a low-cost housing area where the sidewalks were still mostly adobe clay, and the bills were hard to collect. I used a bike borrowed from a neighborhood boy, and on rainy days the thick and sticky adobe quickly choked up my spokes and chain. I had to stop every half block or so and scrape the clay from the fenders with a stick, or wipe off chunks that had spattered my papers.

I loved that San Diego *Union*. Not only because the first press clippings in my scrapbooks came from that paper, but because the job gave me a business experience I could not have learned anywhere else.

Newspaper delivery boys know how to collect money from recalcitrant customers, how to placate an ornery man who's never satisfied with your delivery time and how to keep books. Early in life you learn the complete cycle—the job you have to do rain or shine, complaints or not, in order to please the public and keep the money coming in. And you begin to understand people. There is always a gentle, gray-haired woman in a little white house who is good for a piece of cake or a glass of cold milk. There is an older man who tips you too much, and there's the grumpy man who stalls when you try to collect. There's the pretty young bride who fusses if the paper picks up a smudge of dirt, and the unkempt older wife who, while complaining there is too much crime news, can't wait to see who won the fifth at Hollywood Park.

Newsboys know how to handle them all. And I am sure that right now I could still fold a hundred papers in record time. I am also sure I could toss them unerringly—as newsboys love to do when they're peeved with a subscriber—under trees and porches or on a roof or to some other inaccessible place. If all the "lost" or "undelivered" newspapers in any city were laid end to end, they would make a mighty soggy trail.

Not long after I started my newspaper route, I began to notice for the first time that my father occasionally got official-looking letters bearing Canadian stamps.

When these letters came, my foster parents behaved very strangely. If they were reading them when I came into the room, the conversation was suddenly switched to some innocuous subject. Once or twice, going to my father's room, I saw him poring over a package of these same letters, and the instant he saw me he quickly put them away into a drawer. All children overhear everything—I call this Linkletter's Law of Child Behavior—and are naturally curious about family secrets. I was no different. One day, when I knew my father would be out of the house for hours, I sneaked into his room and examined the forbidden hoard.

Perhaps, like Bluebeard's wife, I made a grave mistake. Perhaps not.

But that was the day I discovered that my real name was Gordon Arthur Kelly, and that I was an adopted child. The adoption papers were there. So were letters from my real parents, asking questions about me. The knowledge that I had another identity in life, and that I had been farmed out by parents who didn't want me was a profound shock.

I did not confront the Linkletters with what I considered a deception. But as I grew older—and I feel even more strongly about it today—I realized that every adopted child should be told the truth at the earliest possible moment. Foster parents should never take the chance that a child will learn the truth accidentally, perhaps in some cruel, taunting way from a playmate.

The fraud is not conceived in love for the child, It is self-love, an attempt to extend one's own personality. The lie—and it is a lie—of pretending the child is your own when he is not will always be exposed. And the exposure might convince such an adopted child that you, the parents, don't tell the truth about anything. The truth is much better. The truth is that you chose this child because you wanted him and that proves your love. The child should know that as soon as he is old enough to understand.

Oddly enough, my first reaction was a strange sense of relief.

I was now able to shrug off all the bitter truths from which there had seemed no escape. Few young boys have a true sense of values, and I was no exception. It galled me that our neighbors thought Father Linkletter was a "queer religious duck"— and they did—and that they considered him a financial failure. I was humiliated by the patched shirts and underwear I put on every day, even though they were scrupulously clean. I was embarrassed by the drunks and gamblers and the other sinners who drifted in and out of our house.

Suddenly all this was changed. Now I could dream.

I was just a temporary guest in the house. The Linkletters were just "stand-in" parents, caring for me until the day my rich, handsome father would come in a shiny limousine and take me home to a mansion where there would be no bums nor borrowed bikes nor Salvation Army cast-off clothes. What a sad, warped dream this was, and the only mitigating circumstance about it is that Father Linkletter, who gave all that he could, never knew what was in my mind at the time.

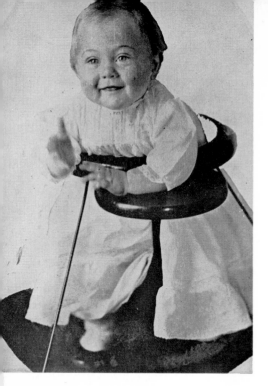

I was a happy baby in this picture, taken in Moose Jaw, the Canadian city where I was born. Years later I was shocked to learn that my real name was Arthur Gordon Kelly and that I had been rejected by my parents shortly after I was born.

In school at San Diego I was skinny and small, but I wanted to be somebody—especially when any cute little blonde girls were around.

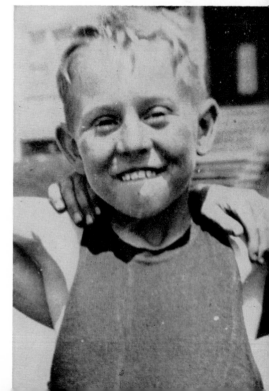

I was adopted in Moose Jaw by John and Mary Linkletter, and they gave me all the love and devotion that they could. When my first son, Jack, was born—and he was very much a wanted baby—they were once more as happy as the day they took me into their home.

I was crazy about a beautiful San Diego girl named Lois Foerster, and there was nothing wrong with her except that she wore her hair in bangs. I told myself that this was a problem that could be solved easily—with scissors. As you can see from this picture, taken on our wedding day, the bangs disappeared, and I never saw them again.

Below, my son Jack and I try each other out for size.

Overwhelmed by the magic of radio, I am making my first broadcast at the Golden Gate International Exposition in San Francisco in 1937.

The jug-eared character at the left in this picture below is my dear friend Clyde Vandeburg, who led me through one world's fair after another. "Keep your eyes off the girls," he said just before the picture was snapped, "and try to look like an executive."

Art Baker and I seem to be a happy combination here during an early "People Are Funny" broadcast, but he wanted to get rid of me—and he did.

Below, my partner John Guedel and I (we dreamed up the "People Are Funny" show together) reminisce about the old days in our Beverly Hills office. The walls are covered with some of our national awards which, in private, we kiddingly call "band-aids to soothe our emotional wounds."

I used to think I was a good actor until I made a movie called "Champagne for Caesar." In that epic drama I was thoroughly clobbered by two old pros named Ronald Colman and Vincent Price.

There are two young ladies who think I am the greatest emcee in the business. They'd better—or I'll cut off their allowance. Meet my daughters—Diane and Sharon—as they appeared on the "House Party" show.

In Hollywood they say Linkletter keeps on having children and grand-children just to make sure he'll always have an audience. And why not? Here I am giving the works to my son Jack, his wife Barbara, and their first baby. The others in the family—and they do come cheaper by the dozen—are always available if I run short.

Purposely picking on a porpoise is one of my favorite weekend sports.
Here I am at Marineland, near Palos Verdes, feeding fish to one of
my pet porpoises. More people lose fingers that way. . . .

Our family doctor once said: "Keep fit and your clothes will always fit." He didn't know of course, that Lois would have a fit, too, when I first started water skiing at forty-five miles an hour.

I may lose friends everywhere if I admit that one of my companies made and sold ten million spin-a-hoops. If it's any comfort to distracted parents, I tested the hoops myself, and there are a couple of kinked vertebrae I still haven't straightened out.

Once a year, I go on the famed Rancheros ride in Santa Barbara, and my horse has to take a beating when I drop my two hundred pounds on his back. I know how the horse feels because I was once a horse myself—as Jack, Dawn, Robert, Sharon and Diane discovered when they wanted a ride.

The only missing links in this happy Linkletter family portrait are the grandchildren. The baby carriages just wouldn't fit on the living room couch. Standing behind me, much too big now for piggyback rides, are Jack, Sharon and Robert. Our lovely Dawn sits on my right, and Lois has her arm around Diane.

My business manager might call this big house "Linkletter's Folly," but what's a man going to do with all those kids around? The gallant gentleman opening the car door for the beautiful lady is me, of course. "Why, Art!" Lois said kiddingly, "you haven't done that for years."

On a lazy Sunday afternoon on our sun porch we're apt to run out of chairs, as Diane has learned. Two new members of the cast are Jack's pretty wife, Bobbie, and their little boy, Mike. Like all the rest of the Linkletters, Mike smiles because he knows the photographer is just about ready to shoot.

Sights you'll never see on the "House Party" show. At the top, having assured son Robert that I was a pretty good lifeguard once, I drag him into the pool.

They used to play the game of volleyball with a ball. But at our house we use little Mike instead, as he is learning to his delight.

My foster father, John Linkletter, often said: "Walk with Jesus, Artie, and you'll never be alone." Last year, all of us took our first trip to the Holy Land. Here, walking along the Nazareth road Jesus often took centuries ago, I paused to tell my children what my father had said so many times.

What can a man write or say when he looks back on twenty-five years of a happy life with the only girl he ever loved? There has been so much. The blue days and the gay days. The magic and misery of show business. The screwballs and the brains. Great men and small. Good men and bad. Wonderful people everywhere. Our hope is that tomorrow may be as rich and happy for everyone as it has been for us.

iii

Not long after I learned the Linkletter family secret, we moved to a house on Euclid Avenue, and I entered the Woodrow Wilson Junior High School.

I was a skinny, undersized boy who seemed to have no talent for anything. I was interested in athletics, especially basketball, but because of my light weight I was limited to the junior teams. There was in me an unrecognized hunger to be somebody, but there was no one then to guide me or push me in any marked direction. At the time, the auditorium for our junior high school was under construction, and once when it was dusk and the carpenters had gone home for the day, I got in through a back door and stood on the stage.

I looked down on row after row of empty seats in this dusty skeleton of a hall, and as the light faded from the windows and the sky turned dark I could hear voices. The sound swelled, and soon the seats were filled, and a sea of faces surged in little waves as the people waited for me to speak. I walked forward as the applause died down to a mere whisper of patting hands, and began my lecture. I was in wonderful voice, and as I talked there were gasps of surprise and spontaneous ripples of sound from the most distant row, and I knew I had this audience with me on every ringing word.

Suddenly a man came out from the wings, and this was the big moment. He had a huge gold cup in his hand—the traditional honor award from the City of San Diego—and my name was engraved on it in letters an inch high.

"Hey, kid!" he said. "What the hell are you doing in here at night?"

The audience melted away and the gold cup turned into a broom. I looked at the school janitor and mumbled: "I was just rehearsing a speech."

"Yeah?" he said. "Well, rehearse it someplace else. Now beat it."

The auditorium was completed a week or two later, but I never gave another ad-lib performance there, with or without an audience. I was not to be denied, however, and I concentrated on my studies to such an extent that many of my fellow students probably thought I was an obnoxious eager beaver.

One semester, the Kiwanis Club offered a fifty dollar prize for the most deserving student. Presently, Principal John Aseltine announced that I had been picked as the winner, and I promptly skipped school to celebrate. I went to a matinee movie theater on Fifth Street—this was a rare indulgence for me, since it cost fifteen cents—and when I came out, whistling happily to myself, a smiling man tapped me on the shoulder.

"You look happy, son," he said. "How come you're not in school?"

I was a cocky youngster and I talked too much, an ailment I have never quite cured. "Mister," I said, "I won a scholarship, and I don't have to be in school today."

"Oh . . ." he said. "You're a special case, eh? What's your name?"

"Art Linkletter," I replied.

The man nodded, and whisked out a card that identified him as a truant officer. I took one horrified look, jumped out of reach and bounded down the street like a rabbit. He caught me, though, and fifteen minutes later I was standing in the principal's office getting the blistering of my young life. "There are some people," Aseltine said gravely, "who think life is a breeze and just can't stand success. I am surprised and disappointed to discover that you seem to be one of those."

He told me bluntly that he was holding up my fifty dollar prize—this was the worst punishment of all—and said he would make a final decision after a six months' probationary period. For fifty dollars I would have changed my name to Little Orphan Annie and behaved accordingly, and eventually I did get the money.

Frankly, I don't know whether Aseltine's scolding had the desired effect or not. I was about thirteen years old, and a thirteen-year-old skin is apt to be pretty thick. But if I missed the point at the time, I had it rammed home for good years later by Jack Benny. I was then a newcomer to Hollywood, and I was invited to join Benny, George Burns and Gracie Allen and several others in a Community Chest benefit show.

I was told that the event would be staged at a Beverly Hills movie theater with three thousand seats, and that it was a priceless opportunity for a young performer. At showtime, when I was given the cue to open the program, I went out front and was stunned to see exactly fourteen people in this vast playhouse. I stood there, appalled by the emptiness, and decided not to exert myself. I made a few perfunctory remarks, and then introduced Benny.

Jack gave me a puzzled look as I brushed past him and he went on stage for his act. "He'll be right back," I said to myself. But he wasn't. He worked his heart out for thirty-five minutes in one of the finest performances of his career, and those fourteen lucky ones in the audience will never forget it. Neither will I.

Jack took me aside and said gently, "You know, Art, when a customer leaves his home and buys a ticket to see you, he's entitled to the best you've got, even if he's the only one in the house." That night I vowed I would never again fail those who came to watch me perform. I like to think this is one promise I have kept.

3. Diagnosis: Girl-Crazy

Milton Berle, at a private banquet in Hollywood: "I predict Art Linkletter will be a great comedian some day. But don't go by me. Ten years ago I predicted Zsa Zsa Gabor would be a Sunday school teacher."

SHOW BUSINESS was the last thing on my mind during my school days. I was much more interested in girls.

When I listen to the old pros nowadays—Berle, Bob Hope, Red Skelton, George Burns and many others—I often wish I had been born in a trunk backstage and had those long years of training which helped make these artists so great. But when they were learning the trade in second-rate theaters, taverns and clubs, I was a high school boy with no particular interest in anything except blondes and a very dubious future. Had Berle seen me then, he might have predicted that I would grow up and go to work for the Kinsey report.

Every small boy with normal instincts begins his research on girls the day his glands start moving the hormones around, and mine must have come to life very early indeed.

I have a distinct and pleasurable recollection of kissing a girl in a swing. I kissed her on the upstroke, and on the down-stroke she gave me a shove and I was catapulted out of the swing nose first. She was obviously not Lolita, but the bruised nose was worth the sensation, and I suspect I felt no pain at all. There was another young girl who, when I kissed her in a barn, ran around in crazy little circles and said she was a bluebird getting ready to nest. The feathers flew around that barn, be-lieve me, but she soon moved away to Hollywood where, I imagine, she probably found a place to roost.

Another time there was a miniature Marilyn Monroe who somehow got me into a coat closet at Junior High School and was teaching me how to nuzzle when who should pop in for a quick cigarette but the teacher. I was suspended for three days, but the little Jezebel wasn't scolded at all.

As my friends know, I am not much of a drinking man. I sip on a cocktail now and then and, as a master of ceremonies, I have been subjected to enough bottles of champagne to make a bubble bath big enough for King Kong. But liquor does nothing for me. It neither sharpens my wit, nor slows me down, and if I am wary about its effect on my circulatory system it is probably because my first drinking experience was a painful jolt.

It happened shortly after I entered San Diego High School, where there was a big, tough, red-headed senior who took fiendish delight in needling me. I went to a school dance one evening—it was the first time I had formally dated a girl—and, like many an adult during the Prohibition days, the more sophisticated boys were enlivening school parties with bootleg booze. During the evening, my tormentor coaxed me to his car with two or three other boys.

"You've always wanted to be a big shot, Linkletter," he said, handing me a silver flask, "so let's see if you're big enough to join us in a drink."

I thought about my girl and how impressed she would be, and I grabbed the flask and took a hefty gulp. But instead of liquor, it was gasoline, and if anyone had lit a match I would have spouted flame. I was not only violently ill, but I was the butt of some cruel jokes around school, and I have been dubious about bottles and flasks ever since. But the worm finally turned. Some ten years later, when I was radio program director for the Dallas Exposition in Texas, who should turn up for an announcer's job but this same scheming red-head. I gave him a nightmare of a tryout, under conditions that turned him into a nervous wreck, and then I hired him. He's been in radio ever since, and it serves him right.

Remembering my high school days, I wonder what any of the girls saw in me. At one time or another, I had suffered every childhood disease known to mothers and medicine—mumps, whooping cough, measles, diphtheria, pneumonia and scarlet fever, and some others I can't spell. It is a strange fact that since high school I have had no health problems at all, and in twenty-five years I have missed only one performance because of illness.

But in school, though I desperately wanted to be a good athlete, I was skinny and scrawny and small. I was never able to make the San Diego High basketball varsity and had to play with the lightweight teams. It was plainly apparent to me that I would never be a lady killer on the courts or playing fields—I simply could not compete with the husky and handsome boys on the varsity—and so I went into other activities where, at least, my name would be known.

I joined the Debating Society and also signed up for the drama class. I am probably remembered by my teachers and fellow students as a boy with a tongue that defied all the laws of perpetual motion. I loved to talk—anywhere, any time, about anything. I still do. I have only been stopped once and

the man who did it was my friend, Groucho Marx. I had admired Groucho's iridescent wit for years—ironically, he is a
fair non-stop windjammer himself—and when he finally invited me to his home for the first time, I was as eager as a
sultan with a new harem. Groucho surrounds himself with
brilliant writers and directors, and I looked forward to an
evening of provocative conversation.

We raced through dinner, moved into the living room and I
waited for Groucho to start things off with some tantalizing
bon mot. He reached into a cupboard for a blackboard and set
it up at one end of the room.

"What's that for?" I asked.

"Word games," he said. "We're going to play word games."

I sat in a corner for the next two hours, chewing my thumb
while they fooled around with note pads and the blackboard,
and not one man in this collection of keen minds opened his
mouth to talk about show business or politics or books. I
could scarcely get one conversational word in, and I have
never been so frustrated before or since. Groucho later told
me that he and his guests had been close friends for years,
and they played acrostics and other word games as a gym-
nastic exercise for their minds.

Garrulous as I was in school, there was no flash of genius in
my conversation, and the teachers were not excited about me.
Judging by their biographies, most of my contemporaries in
show business had stage ambitions in their early teens, or their
talents cropped out while they were still in short pants. The-
atrical agents—or ten percenters, as we call them—were signing them to contracts almost before they learned to write. Some
of them still can't write. But no one was pursuing me, not even
the girl next door. Matter of fact, there was no girl next door.
Had there been such a girl I would have been pursuing her.

I was a baby-faced, innocent-looking kid in high school, and consequently the drama teacher was always casting me in little-boy parts. "You've got a sad wistful look about you," they said, "and you'll get sympathy in these roles." Finally, when I threatened to quit, I was cast as a detective in a murder mystery.

When the great moment came, shortly after the curtain rose, I got flustered and blurted out the cue line I was not supposed to use until the last act. My blooper revealed to the audience who "done it," and the suspense was ruined. I was given a flunking grade for the course, and I had the distinct impression that the teachers were relieved when I decided the theater was not for me. A couple of years later, by the way, another boy at San Diego High played the same role so superbly that he got an A-plus. His name was Gregory Peck.

ii

My emotional problems at school were rarely discussed at home. I had no real father-and-son closeness with John Link-letter, at least not the kind of adventures I have had with my own boys. He was hopelessly beyond my reach—all his time was devoted to the Lord and not much else—and while we respected and loved each other, neither of us knew how to give complete affection and understanding. He rarely gave me any advice without quoting the Bible, and when I needed him most he seemed preoccupied and remote.

Once in a while, especially when I watched him at work in his little cobbler shop, I got rewarding glimpses of a man I could love and understand. He became a cobbler, I'm sure, because he always fought against pride within himself, and in the repairing of other people's shoes he would be performing humble work. He had great manual dexterity, and he took pleasure in even the smallest job. He bought the best leathers and threads, and when a shoe was shaped and stitched and polished he would hold it up to the light, and his eyes shone.

One day he saw me watching this little ritual. "Artie," he said, "always do a good job as best you know how. When you grow up, pick a job you like, otherwise you won't do it well. Like me, for instance. I *like* to mend shoes."

Perhaps he was deluding himself. I know that he was much happier standing beneath a tree in one of San Diego's parks, where he often walked, and talking about the Lord to anyone who would listen. He had great personal courage with his faith, too, and I recall one simmering afternoon when he came upon a horse that had dropped on the street and was being viciously whipped by the driver.

There was a crowd of bystanders watching this cruel performance, but no man interfered. My father exploded, grabbed the wagoner's shirt and threw him to the ground. The man was twice his size, but Father said: "If you hurt that horse again I'll put the whip to you myself." The man was awed by my father's righteous anger, and promised to be kind to the animal.

Characteristically, Father went home and prayed that he would be forgiven his raging impulse.

But he had a blind spot when it came to solving my conflicts and disappointments and mistakes. Young boys who cannot find spiritual and material help at home usually look for a substitute father, and I found mine at the San Diego YMCA. His name was Dave Bomberger, an effervescent young man who was physical director there, and who also supervised an intramural club called The Friendly Indians. I wanted to be a Friendly Indian, too, and Bomberger helped me win a membership in the club.

I had learned to swim along the waterfront at San Diego and San Pedro, where the water was dirty and choppy and often contaminated with oil, and the best I can say for my stroke is that it was good enough to push floating beer bottles or drifting lumber out of the way. Consequently, when I first saw the clear water in the Y pool, I needed no urging from Bomberger to try competitive swimming, and one proud day I won the Southern California fifty-yard backstroke championship.

When I was not busy swimming or playing basketball, I worked at the Y.

I gathered up the soggy towels in the locker room, and helped coach younger boys in the pool. I worked on the desk where I learned a modern Confucianism that saved me thousands of dollars in later years: *Never cash checks for pleading young men who say they were rolled in Agua Caliente.*

I ran the mimeograph machine, among other things, mailing out club notices, bills and announcements, and I estimate that I licked ten thousand stamps. I can still taste the glue—it wasn't as sweet as the stuff the government uses today—and one of my first extravagances when I opened an office in Hollywood years later was a stamping machine that did the licking for me.

The San Diego Y was also the scene of what might be called the first Linkletter broadcast, though there is no plaque to mark the site, and they would have fired me had they known what was going on.

I often worked the switchboard for the Y hotel and, being insatiably curious, I listened in when some of the older fellows were phoning their girls. Later, when the board was quiet, I would plug in three or four of my younger pals and dramatize the intimate conversations I had overheard. It was not very sporting, I guess, but this eavesdropping did give me an early and somewhat spicy course on the facts of life. Some of those older men (they must have been all of nineteen or twenty) had some fascinating hunting techniques when they were pursuing a reluctant young lass, and my father would have been shocked,

I'm sure, if he had known that knowledge about the biological chase is not always acquired from books.

Long afterward, when my own children reached the teens and became phone addicts, there were times when, in a hurry to make an important call, I inadvertently cut in on some of their personal talk. It was pretty obvious that they considered me a snooper even when I protested that my business calls came first. I solved the problem, though, as many another distracted parent has done. I gave them a phone of their own and nobody—but nobody—has any excuse for cutting into their line.

iii

During summers I served as a counselor at the Y camp in the southern California mountains, near the town of Julian, and worked there with hundreds of boys. A souvenir I treasure was a photograph sent to me by one of the grateful mothers. It was a picture of me with several small boys who were learning how to use a baseball bat. One of these lads—and we have since laughed about how lean and skinny he was at the time—was the boy who became the "Splendid Splinter," Ted Williams of the Boston Red Sox. I like to think that our rigorous outdoor training program taught Ted how to keep in shape, and I note that as this is written he has just hit his 520th home run, at the age of forty-two.

I have often tried to trace down the day and hour when I picked up the show-business virus. Perhaps it was always there, dormant. The plug-in arrangement on the hotel switchboard was a beginning but this was more fourteen-year-old mischief than anything else.

My first planned broadcast, as nearly as I can remember,

took place at Camp Marston on July 26, 1928. That day Gene Tunney, then the heavyweight champion, was fighting Tom Heeney at the Yankee Stadium in New York. It was to be Tunney's last appearance in the ring, though Tunney had not made any formal announcement about retiring, and the bout was to be broadcast.

I was in charge of the daily campfire shows that summer—inventing stunts similar to those I later used on People Are Funny—but the fight broadcast was a very special event for us, of course, and it gave me an idea. One of the boys at camp had a small hand microphone, another owned an amplifying unit. We hooked this equipment to a radio receiver and tuned in the fight program.

Along about the sixth or seventh round, when I thought I had heard enough to imitate the announcer at ringside in New York, we cut off the network broadcast and I took over with my hand mike. I was hidden behind a cottage and I faked some five or six rounds of the fight so vividly, or so I was told later, that the kids around the campfire never knew the difference. I had both warriors staggering around the ring, bloody, glassy-eyed and I got to a screaming, breathless finish as Tunney was hit with a crashing left hook and went down for the count.

Unfortunately, as I learned the next morning, the New York fight ended quite differently. Tunney knocked out Heeney in the eleventh round, and the boys at camp who had collected their winnings the night before—they had all made bets, of course—had to give the money back. I was considered a deceiving villain for a couple of days, and the kids who had been tricked failed to appreciate Linkletter's ad-lib skill at the mike.

Years later, when I was already a pro at Station KGB in San Diego and had learned that faked broadcasts are considered highly unethical, I was assigned to cover the arrival of the Pacific Fleet. The San Diego Exposition was then attracting thousands of visitors every day, and the Navy had guaranteed to bring in this mighty fleet as a special event which we could put on the CBS national network.

At ten o'clock that morning, I stood on the Municipal Pier, microphone in hand, scanning a list of the ships that would be parading down the bay. Around me, happily awaiting the return of their men to the base, were hundreds of Navy wives and sweethearts, to say nothing of a yelling phalanx of children. At ten-fifteen, some forty-five minutes before we were due to go on the air, we were hit with the first soft spray of an offshore fog. The long gray bank, thick as wallpaper paste, moved in across the bay and by ten-thirty there was no visibility at all.

Shivering in this wet mist, I was handed a Navy message which said that the Admiral of the Fleet refused to risk coming into the harbor until the fog lifted. It might take an hour or two.

At ten fifty-five, the fog was so dense that I could barely make out the frowning face of Clyde Vandeburg, promotion director for the Exposition. He was stomping up and down the pier, cussing the weather, and I said: "We'll never make it, Van."

"The Devil we won't," he snapped. "Every businessman in town has money in this fair, and besides, if we cancel on account of fog, the Chamber of Commerce will run us out of town."

"But the fog—?"

"Fog or no fog," he said, "you're going to bring in the Fleet."

At eleven, exactly, I was on the air. I described battleships I had never seen. I talked about men standing at attention on the decks of cruisers which, for all I knew, might be running aground at that very moment. Somewhere offshore, the Fleet Admiral, listening to my excited voice, was banging on his desk and using language rarely seen in print, and at the pier rival reporters and photographers were frantically wondering what kind of magic equipment helped me see ships still miles out of sight.

We went off the air as the last of my ghostly vessels tied up at their docks. "Heeney wins again," I said to Van.

"What?" he asked. "I don't get it."

"Oh, it's just an old Linkletter password," I said.

I had gotten away with the most blatant fraud ever perpetrated on a coast-to-coast show. I know I got away with it because the Navy didn't come up with even one small squawk. They were not going to confess that the skippers of these great battle wagons—survivors of the deadliest storms—were unwilling to come home in a fog. The newspapers and other radio stations would not admit we had a three-hour beat on the news, and the CBS officials said nothing because they didn't know the program was faked. Indeed, I waited years before I confessed to them what I had done that day.

If my love affair with radio began with Tunney and Heeney that July day at the Y camp—and I am sure it did—I have to credit an assist to an ingenious gentleman named Emile Berliner. Not one person in a thousand has ever heard his name, but Berliner invented the microphone, and without this remarkable gadget there would have been no Art Linkletter on the air. Whether this is good or bad for the nation depends on your point of view, but the instrument has been Aladdin's lamp for me.

I had no precocious understanding about the powers of this simple instrument, of course, and another five years would pass before the union was consummated.

I was not quite seventeen when I was graduated from San Diego High in June, 1929—barely out of adolescence and plainly immature. I was still so baby-faced and fuzzy-cheeked that I felt insecure about going on to college with older boys, and I had not decided what I wanted to do in life. San Diego suddenly seemed narrow and confining to me, and I wanted to make a break. I was ready to go anywhere, with no particular itinerary in mind.

It never occurred to me that I was running away from home, or that this would be a flight from reality.

I told myself that I wanted to see other places and people, and that I would thus be better prepared for college. I could not have defined it at the time, but the real motivation was probably an urge to prove to the Linkletters and my real parents, wherever they were, that I, the unwanted, adopted boy, didn't need them any more. I may not have realized it, but the chip-on-the-shoulder belligerency was there, and with any other family background I might very well have turned to a neighborhood gang for the lift I needed. I once asked Archie Moore, the great and ageless boxing champion, how he overcame the transgressions that blighted his boyhood years. "Simple, Art," he said. "I grew up." I wanted to grow up, too.

On July 15, 1929, with ten dollars in my pocket, I went out on my own.

4. Diary of a Teen-Ager

There was a seven-year-old boy on my House Party show one morning, and I asked him which of the fairy tales he liked best.

"The one about the three bears," he said.

"That's a good one," I said. "What does it teach you?"

"Lock your door when you go out," he said, "or else you might find a girl in your bed."

THERE WAS NO little Goldilocks wandering around my house when I finished high school, and I certainly never found one in my bed.

This was probably just as well, remembering how the chemicals were surging around in my tissues at the time. I might easily have been coaxed into some form of steady employment to meet the inevitable overhead of young love. But I had locked my door. Behind me was a childhood with few sweet memories and there were no umbilical attachments to either of my foster parents. This was not my fault, nor theirs. There was a hurried good-bye, and Dad told me to be a good boy. Mother, with tears in her eyes, said she'd pray for me. They could not foresee, and neither could I, that I would never live with them again.

Denver Fox, a boy about my own age whom I had known

and liked at school and camp, went with me on my aimless tour.

I kept a daily diary—I had it retyped just the other day because it was faded and torn—and a nostalgic re-reading suggests that it was on this long journey that I first realized that People Are Funny.

Among other things, we learned to chisel rides on freight trains, outwit the railroad bulls, cook stews with the bindle stiffs and never argue with a gun. I was in a boxcar near Missoula, Montana, when a thug with a .32 stuck up all the bums—including Denver and me—and put a slug through one man's leg because he didn't move fast enough. I've been leery of guns ever since, and I jump like a pogo stick every time the villain gets his on the television set at home.

We started our trip standing thumbs up on the coast highway between Los Angeles and San Francisco, and we were lucky. Thirty years ago, motorists were not as suspicious of young hitchhikers as they are today—there had not been as many ruthless highway murders, I suppose—and we got so many rides that we reached San Francisco, some four hundred and fifty miles from home, the second day.

I note that when we left San Francisco I wrote in my diary: "I don't believe I like 'Frisco. Too old, dirty, uniform and foggy." This will be disillusioning news to my friend Mayor George Christopher of the Golden Gate city, considering that my radio and television career struck gold in San Francisco, that I learned to love the people, that I still pay taxes there, and that during the long years I lived there I indignantly chopped up any visiting oafs who came on my program and called it " 'Frisco."

Traveling north on the Redwood Highway, Denver and I slept in barley fields, haylofts, under the redwood trees or any other place that was handy when we were tired. On the fourth morning, half awake in a field some miles north of Eureka, I saw a pair of big brown eyes gazing tenderly at me. I dreamed she was an Oriental princess and reached out to embrace her. At that point, she gave me a whack with her swishing tail, and I opened my eyes to discover that she was no lady at all but only a nosy cow.

As literature, I'm afraid my diary will not have the immortality of Samuel Pepys's journal. The sensations and emotions, the sights and sounds on its pages mirror the primitive delights and surprises that would be important to most any seventeen-year-old boy. The philosophy is what you might expect from a naïve, unsophisticated small-town lad who had never run much beyond the limits of his leash. The approach is wide-eyed and joyous. Some sample excerpts during the first month out:

> July 19—We came to Patrick's Creek Tavern, in the Smith River Country, a high class hotel and eating house, and bought some candy bars. On the way out, a couple of ladies who were walking toward us said: "Hello, boys." We started talking to them. Then, without even a hint, one of them told us to go in and order a big dinner on her. She gave us each a dollar. As we were sitting at the table the one lady's companion told me to go outside as the other lady wanted to see me. I did go, and she gave me $5 for both of us! ! ! Boy, boy, surprised? Pleased? I'll say so.
>
> July 23—We expect to get a freight tonight. After getting dressed and eating, we hung around the depot for a while. A road bull came up and threatened us with 30 days in jail. Being green we were fooled and he made us buy 2 train tickets to Pendleton.
>
> July 26—Got an N.P. freight out about 2 P.M. and rode the rest of the day on a big lumber gondola.
>
> We are certainly meeting strange characters on the road. On this car there is a guy with St. Vitus dance, a

Los Angeles clerk, a New York gangster, a miner, a lumberjack, a young tough from Chi, and three tough kids from Butte.

July 27—Denver just did something that was a bit unwise but it might turn out all right. He loaned his heavy sweater to a guy who had nothing on but a shirt. That is humane, but unwise among bums. However, one can never tell.

July 28—All the bums came back, all except the guy with the sweater. So it turned out wrong after all.

July 29—We just passed Butte, Montana, a town reputed for its hardness in a company of hard men, so it must be bad.

August 1—Arrived in Minneapolis today. Went to the Y, took a shower and a nice long swim. Went to an employment agency and applied for jobs as bus boys. Had to explain to Denver that a bus boy is not one who carries suitcases from busses into hotels.

On second thought, perhaps I shouldn't have had the diary retyped.

I note, though, that we worked several weeks as bus boys in a Minneapolis dive, intriguingly named Le Chat Noir, which operated as a roadhouse. The joint was packed with low-grade celebrants defying prohibition, and they not only used up all the oxygen with cigarettes and cigars, but burned holes in the tablecloths. I have studiously avoided night clubs and cigarettes ever since, and when I make the rare exception something invariably happens to prove that I'm not such a square after all.

Six years ago, for instance, I reluctantly agreed to attend a Hollywood nightclub party for a visiting Texas oil millionaire. I was sitting at a table with Miss Marie (The Body) McDonald and her then husband, Harry Karl. Someone dropped a lighted cigarette and the burning end touched twenty or thirty yards of pink and mauve tulle that was attached to Marie. There was a sudden eye of flame and Marie saw herself doing a strip-tease with fire. I sat there pop-eyed, I'm afraid, because you don't often see this kind of an act, but her husband beat out the flames before the finale.

Someone might have blamed me for plotting this as a People Are Funny stunt, but fortunately no one has ever seen me puff on a cigarette. Indeed, I was sponsored by a tobacco company for years, and I stubbornly refused to hold a cigarette, or puff one to pretend I smoked. I explained to a top executive of the company that I didn't smoke, and didn't approve of smoking. To my surprise he said: "Neither do I."

Denver Fox and I worked in and around Minneapolis and St. Paul until October 5.

I was a bellboy at the Curtis Hotel, an usher at the State and Century Theaters, a tray washer at Wrigley's Restaurant, a welder and sheet metal helper. I reached Minneapolis with $1.50 in my pocket and left there with $52.50 and a couple of pawnshop suits. We made New York City in six days, hitching rides on cars and trucks, including one two-hundred-mile stretch during which we sat atop a load of caskets. "Ha-ha. First time I've ever hauled two live stiffs," the driver said. "Some joke, huh?" When Denver and I failed to laugh, the trucker frowned. "Look," he explained, "you guys are on the bum. A bum is a bindle stiff, see, and . . . oh . . . the hell with it." He dropped us outside Buffalo, and his day was ruined.

ii

In the textbooks for fathers, with such titles as "What Every Boy Should Know" or "How to Raise Your Son to Manhood," there are profound sermons on such things as the danger of going into the woods with a girl and so on, but I have never seen any advice pro or con on the value of hitting the road.

The psychologists might argue that a boy can handle what he's ready for, including ladies of the night or men with nervous trigger fingers, but that not all seventeen-year-olds would benefit from this kind of baptism. I don't know about the others. I only know what happened to me. I was a boy when I left home, a man when I got to New York.

Physically I was taller and stronger; mentally and emotionally, I had found new capacities within myself.

Along the route I met hundreds of people—scoundrels and heroes, laborers and bosses, geniuses and nitwits—and there was not one who did not have something to give. I learned that no man has to starve if he's willing to work, and that you make your own horizons. Best of all, my mind was storing up countless little facts about people which would later be useful on my radio and television shows.

Francis Bacon once said: "Travel, in the younger set, is a part of education; in the elder, a part of experience." For me it was both. There were chuck holes here and there, of course, but the stumbles they caused left only minor bruises.

I recall a New York doctor who needed a secretary, and I thought I could do the job. Knowing he would require shorthand, I spent a couple of days working out some hieroglyphics of my own. But the medic was one of those shooting gallery dictators—bang, bang—and all I got on paper was a preposition here and there. I got a proposition from the doctor's nurse, too, and I was never quite sure whether I was fired for that or my home-made shorthand.

There was another enlightening experience when I was working as a clerk in the National City Bank in New York. Anyone old enough will remember that the stock market disintegrated in October, 1929, and I was at the bank when you could barely get down the street without being hit by brokers jumping out of forty-story buildings.

At that point, one of my employers—a shrewd, cautious operator if there ever was one—scraped up every nickel he owned and invested them all in a so-called blue-ribbon stock that couldn't possibly go any lower. I withdrew the $196 I had saved and cleverly bought some of the same stock. Four years later I sold it for eight dollars—an expensive way to learn the lesson about putting all your eggs in one basket. I don't know what happened to my former boss.

I was in New York from October 11, 1929, until May 15, 1930. In my diary there is a footnote which reads: "Marie, Nanette, Claudine, Iris, Midge, Ruthie, Goldie." I haven't the slightest idea what it means. Maybe they were fillies running at Aqueduct Park and some friend gave me those names as good bets.

Denver and I sailed out of New York on May 16 as ordinary seamen—cadets, we called ourselves—aboard the steamer American Legion. We worked on the vessel for the long round trip to Buenos Aires and Rio de Janeiro, and were initiated into the order of Neptunus Rex as we crossed the Equator. My diary, referring to the victims of this ritual, says: "They were read their various sins and were duly swabbed and anointed with various pastes, rotten eggs, etc. One old fellow they undressed only had a pair of rayon underwear on, and oh, oh! A good time was had by all."

The exact details of what happened to the gentleman with the rayon undies are not important—indeed, they may be censorable—but it was a denouement that had his shipmates in hysterics. Years later, when my partner, John Guedel, and I created the People Are Funny show, we had the problem of finding a gimmick for the audience warmup. This is an informal half-hour period preceding the actual show when we kid around with the audience and try to have them rocking with laughter just as we go on the air. I would like to say modestly that our studio audience was always whooping wildly at that important moment, but our viewers and listeners never knew what had triggered this explosion. I can reveal now that it was really quite simple—a visual gag salvaged from my South American trip. We had John's father, Walter Guedel, walk on stage to give the cue to begin—he had the conservative clothes and serious mien of a professor—and as he solemnly raised one hand his pants fell down.

In my scrapbook there is a long clipping from the San Diego *Union* about our journey to Buenos Aires, and the reporter who interviewed us wrote: "During that visit the boys were able to comb the city's interesting spots thoroughly, their knowledge of the Spanish language, learned while in high school, proving a great aid." This news is clear evidence that you can't believe what you read in the papers, because someone fibbed.

My recollection is that I barely staggered through the Spanish course in high school, and that I flunked it miserably in Buenos Aires. It is true, though, that we combed the city's interesting spots thoroughly, and my diary makes a note of that fact. "We saw most of the town and the race track. Girls we know well are Dora, Elena, Paula, Dolores and Frenchy. Elena is the best of the lot. None of them speak English, just a word or two." We combed around for ten days, and sailed away on Friday the thirteenth. It was an unlucky day for some, as my diary reports: "Denver had his pocket picked of 20 pesos. We finished scraping and varnishing the bridge."

We were in Rio de Janeiro, too, but I'm afraid my diary notes on this city would not do for the travel promotion ads. I gave the town three lines: "Went ashore and saw the strangest sight I've ever seen. The famous whore house district. Fifteen hundred whores in a space of ten blocks! It was some sight! Just a business with them." (Luckily, they scared both of us back to the ship.)

Denver and I started hitchhiking west from New York on July 10, almost a year after we had left home.

Eight days later, after half a dozen auto rides and a small ruckus with a railroad dick who pulled us off a freight train and let us go with a bawling out, we were back in California. The Linkletters, as I had learned from their letters, had moved from San Diego to Visalia. We paused there on the southward turn from Reno to Los Angeles, caught up on the family news, and then hitched a ride to San Diego.

I really regretted leaving the Linkletters, but after a year in an outside world my father had never explored, my life with them would have been restless and unfulfilled. My father never read my diary, and so he could not have known what was in my heart. But I knew.

5. In This Corner: "Kid Lightning"

> *The average small boy (or girl) has daydreams about what he wants to be when he grows up that would dazzle any vocational guidance counselor. I remember one lad in particular on the House Party show who took me into his confidence about his plans for the future.*
>
> *"What do you want to be when you grow up?" I asked him.*
>
> *"A preacher."*
>
> *"Why?"*
>
> *" 'Cause my dad's a preacher."*
>
> *"What does he do most of the time?"*
>
> *"He talks Christians into being Methodists."*

It isn't every boy who knows early what he wants to do for the rest of his life.

In the fall of 1930, after a late summer's work at the Y camp, I had a critical decision to make. Unlike the boy on the House Party show, I was not interested in following in my father's footsteps and becoming a preacher—or even a cobbler. But I did think there was a stimulating future in teaching.

I had enjoyed working with boys at the Y camps—there were so many who needed and got a guiding hand—and I had learned from my travels that thousands of youngsters like me were poorly prepared for the tough business of surviving in a competitive world. But I couldn't teach without a college degree, and college was a formidable challenge when it came to money for tuition, room and board. I registered at San Diego State College in mid-September, and I knew I would have to earn my way.

I hadn't the remotest idea where I would live, and had no money for rent. I thought of sleeping in the Y gym as I had done on the road. Just before school started, though, I was invited to live at the Fox home. Guy Fox was a plumbing contractor who had six sons—Denver was one—and I became a sort of seventh son in this busy and crowded household. But there was still the problem of money for tuition.

Not too long ago I had an urgent letter from the late C. E. Peterson, then the distinguished and admired Dean of Men at San Diego State. He knew I remembered my college days with affection, and he reminded me that there are always deserving young men and women who need help from scholarship funds. He suggested I might like to donate some money annually for scholarships, and to emphasize the need, he enclosed what he called a "typical" letter from an impoverished student who had been helped along the way.

The letter came as a surprise, since of late I hadn't given much thought to the school. My white cells were putting up resistance, as they often do when someone puts the bite on me.

But I read the letter he sent, and I thought it was pretty corny. It was a masterpiece of the poignant pitch, and I wondered how it had ever gotten past the eagle eyes of the scholarship fund committee. I waded through two pages of this hard sell commercial from the student—and when I got to the end I knew Dean Peterson had me. The letter was signed "Art

Linkletter." I sent a check by return mail, and four students each year since then have been helped by the twenty-year-old letter that boomeranged.

The money from the scholarship fund gave me cash for books and other things now and then, and I was never pressed for room and board expenses because Guy Fox refused to let me pay. Even so, I never seemed to have enough.

I learned very soon, from other students who had been doing it for years, that I could pick up a fast ten dollars by selling a pint or two of blood to San Diego doctors and hospitals. I was dropping in for these needle jobs almost once a month—the drain on my arteries never seemed to bother me much—and the ten dollars went a long way toward necessary expenses, such as an occasional soda fountain date with some campus queen. I was reminded of my blood-selling sideline some years later when in Hollywood I met the late Bela Lugosi, who gained movie fame in the role of the sinister Count Dracula. "Too bad you couldn't have worked for me," he said with his familiar vampire leer. "At the studio we were paying young girls two hundred dollars a week—heh, heh—to let me suck the life blood out of their necks."

"Call me when you're making the sequel, Bela," I joked. "I'll pay *you* two hundred a week to let me take your place."

In between blood lettings, I continued working out at the Y gym, and once in awhile I put on boxing gloves with a boy named Lee Ramage. We were sparring around the ring one day when a gentleman with a cauliflower ear and a face like a plowed field asked me to step off into a corner for a little chat.

"Look, kid," he said, "you got a pretty good pair o' mitts. They're puttin' on fights across the border at Tiajuana every weekend, and you could make yourself some dough."

"But that would make me a pro," I said, "and I'd never qualify for any of the teams at school."

"They'll never know," he said. "We'll give you a phony name. How about it?"

I stewed over this proposition for a couple of days and then, learning that some of my friends had already signed up, I agreed to go. The following Sunday, wearing borrowed purple trunks and using the name of "Kid Lightning from Long Beach," I went into the Tiajuana ring for a three-round fight with a young Mexican pro. At the sound of the bell he shot across the ring and belted me on the nose so hard I bounced two feet off the ropes. This boy was *faster* than sound, and he worked me over like an egg-beater. When I tried to hit him he just wasn't there, and at the end of three rounds I was flat on my back and thoroughly scrambled.

I wobbled down out of the ring with my bruises and bloody nose and asked the promoter for my money.

So my amateur standing was untarnished.

"I told ya you'd get paid only if you looked good in there," he said. "But you ain't got it, boy, and I can't use ya."

I never put on boxing gloves again, but Lee Ramage, one boy who didn't go to Tiajuana, continued his training with others at the Y, and eventually became one of the great boxers of his time. He was ahead on points in his first fight with Joe Louis—until Joe lowered the boom on him.

It seems logical to think that the clobbering I got at Tiajuana could have stifled any future interest I might develop in the sport of boxing. On the contrary, I have always been a fight fan, and the fact that a little Mexican buzzsaw cut me to pieces has only increased my admiration for fighters who are clever with their hands. I prefer outdoor fights, though, because at the indoor bouts I am usually knocked out in the first round by cigar smoke.

ii

It is conceivable that this cigar-smoke aversion began when I found a weekend job that was far less strenuous, and infinitely more exciting, than having my veins pumped out or getting chopped up in the ring. One of my friends on the San Diego State campus was John Crofton, a younger brother of Jim and Ern Crofton, who owned and operated the gambling casino at Agua Caliente. This luxurious resort, then known as the Monte Carlo of America, was across the border south of San Diego, and through John I was hired to be a shill there.

Every Saturday afternoon I dusted off my decrepit old Dodge and hoped it would live long enough to make the twenty-five-mile trip to Caliente. There was no starter for the engine, and I had to use a hand crank. There was a time, until I got it fixed, when this evil automobile took an almost human delight in raising my blood pressure. I would give the crank a quick spin to start the motor, then leap into the seat to adjust the choke to keep it going. Most of the time I lost. The engine coughed and died before I could reach the choke, and I wouldn't have put up with this time and again if I had any other means of getting to work. Worse yet, in a heavy rain the hood leaked badly and the dripping water would kill the motor. I solved this drawback by carrying a stack of newspapers on the seat, stuffing them under the hood and setting them on fire. The quick heat dried out the engine, and I could get going again, assuming the car itself wouldn't blow up.

I recall one afternoon when, already late, I chugged into a gas station with my burning newspapers trailing a plume of smoke. The horrified attendant, whose station tanks had just been filled with a thousand gallons of gas, galloped out white-faced and jerked up the hood.

"Hey, what are you doing?" I yelled.

"What d'ya think?" he screamed, aiming the water hose at my motor. "I'm keeping you and me from being blasted to hell and back."

"You killed my engine," I said accusingly. "Now I'll have to light another fire in there."

"Mister," he said with a very penetrating look, "you must be nuts!"

Perhaps I was.

My assignment at the gambling casino was simple enough. I posed as a rich but dissolute college boy who had the gambling fever and was blowing his inheritance at the crap tables. The house would give me three or four hundred dollars, and while I was shooting dice I was to look for evidence of collusion between the croupiers and the players. The pit bosses knew they were being clipped, but they needed proof. If I lost while playing they would give me more money. If I won I had to turn in the winnings. I knew very well that while I was watching them, somebody was watching me.

My pay was fifteen dollars a night, plus room and board at the Agua Caliente Hotel. Considering what I saw and learned there, it would have paid me to work for nothing.

I stood at the tables in the main gambling room four or five weekends in a row. I can still see and smell the drifting white veils of cigar smoke and perhaps that's the place where it first bothered me, but it was an occupational hazard I had to take. Like the yokels who get pop-eyed at the nude girlie shows in Las Vegas nowadays, I was just as awed in this hard, glittering world of gamblers, tourists, celebrities and fools.

Playing alongside me were some of the most solid citizens of

San Diego—businessmen and bankers—and many a roll turned out to be worth ten years in San Quentin. I would read the papers later and see their names front-paged as bankrupts, suicides or embezzlers.

Agua Caliente was also the weekend playground of the wealthy Hollywood stars—these were the great names who got it when income taxes were low—and, in the kinship that unites fellow victims around a crap table, I found myself being friendly and intimate with stars who wouldn't have given me a nod on a Hollywood set.

I remember being introduced to an unknown Mexican girl who was making a name for herself as a dancer. She was then Senorita Margarita Cansino, but now she is better known as Rita Hayworth. At the table—stubbornly betting on number eleven and always losing—was Miss Jean Harlow, the platinum-haired siren of the times, who had not long to live. Clara Bow, the original "It" girl, was another player who never seemed to win, and who soon disappeared from the Hollywood scene.

Clark Gable was there, too. Gable and I, who are now good friends, were reminiscing one recent day about those weekends at Caliente and he laughingly said: "Ah—those were the wild days." I'm sure I don't have to make the point that neither of us is wild any more. I have five children—that's enough to tame any man—and Gable spends his nights at home on a San Fernando Valley ranch. Gable's attitude toward life—and how it has changed in thirty years!—is that he'd rather have a new tractor than a row of Oscars he couldn't use. The best one-line editorial I have ever heard came from Gable during our conversation about Caliente. He was about to leave for Hong Kong to make a picture, and I mentioned the fact that Hong Kong tailors make wonderful suits at bargain prices. "I already have a suit," Gable said.

I imagine Gable had fifty suits during the period he was

going to Caliente for holiday fun, whereas I, gaily scattering twenty-dollar chips that didn't belong to me, was lucky to have one. But the table men at the casino were too busy with their stick work to notice what I wore, and of course I was careful not to let them see me driving my wheezing old car. As the weeks passed, the croupiers lost some of their chilly aloofness with me, and they began to treat me as a young friend who was making a fool of himself.

"Listen," one of them finally said, "why dontcha get outa here and stay out? You'll lose all your dough, they'll throw you outa school and your old man'll cut you out of his will."

"You should talk," I countered. "I notice that every night when this joint closes at two, you and the other guys go over to the Foreign Club and play there all night."

"That's different," he said. "We're pros. We know when to push the luck and when to quit. But you don't."

I kept on playing, of course—feeling like a Fifth Columnist who would soon betray them—and before long they got careless. I noticed that two of the assistant chefs from the kitchen were coming out to play during their off-hours and two of the croupiers were obviously in on the deal. They juggled chips and bets so skillfully that the cooks were making a killing, and I was finally able to turn in a detailed report. The following weekend, the guilty dice men had mysteriously vanished. So had the cooks. I hope they have since gone into some other business far away because now that I've confessed I would not care to have them perforate me on a dark street.

In recent years, some of my eager Hollywood friends, knowing that I was once a shill, and also that I am supposed to have a fair-sized bank account, occasionally lure me into card games at their homes. It is not very flattering to be considered a pigeon, but I comfort myself with the thought that their scheming is a waste of time. When some player raises me five dollars I turn pale, and if it's a ten dollar hike I am apt to faint. When it comes to stud poker, where you have to bet on each turn of a card, I am virtually ready for the embalmer. I learned long ago in Caliente that gambling is for suckers, and the lesson seems to have stayed with me.

I was busier than a rooster in a chicken house during my years at San Diego State, but the experience would be a blur had I not kept a scrapbook. Ah, the vanity of man, who can create his own immortality with scissors and paste. But if I had no scrapbook, I would have to get the information from old classmates all over the world, and there is no knowing what lies they would tell.

My dog-eared notes show that I stayed with the Fox family for a year, and then went to live with another school friend, Gordon Samuel, and his family.

I could have remained at the Fox home indefinitely—Denver's father and mother assured me that I was like one of their own—but I didn't want to overstay my welcome. They were already feeding six husky boys, and the food I stowed away must have been a low blow to their budget. But Gordon was an only son, and his father could help a young student along without a strain on his purse.

Gordon's father was a building contractor who was putting up modestly-priced homes on a speculation basis. He always built the garage first, and we would all live and sleep in this confined space, like Indians in a tepee, until the main house was finished. We would move in to give it a homey and occupied look, and the house would then be offered for sale. Mr. Samuel did so well with this system that there were times when the new house was sold while we were still roughing it in the garage. Nowadays, when I hear the overworked word "togetherness," I get a little twitch. We had it, but it was fun.

iii

My craving for self-expression—and it was insatiable—led to what I euphemistically call the literary phase of my college days.

Walter Winchell was just beginning to achieve fame as a syndicated columnist at the time, and I was brash enough to think that I had similar talents which my classmates would soon discover. I had always wanted to write, and in my daydreams I could see those magic words "by Art Linkletter" leaping from the pages of newspapers and magazines. At one point in my life—and this was not too long ago—a reporter asked me what person I would like to be in my next life, assuming I got through this one. "Quentin Reynolds," I said. It so happens that I have never met this popular writer, but I have admired his work. The name Quentin Reynolds has a wonderful lyrical sound and suggests a tall, handsome man of distinction, reflectively puffing on a pipe and signing autographs for lovely young girls who would be happy to look over his etchings. Indeed, in my reincarnation I would be glad to be Quentin Reynolds-with-etchings even though I never wrote a word.

At San Diego State, we had a college publication called *The Aztec*, romantically named after the Mexican Indians who had absolutely nothing to do with San Diego.

I was listed on the staff as a feature writer. A journalism professor once tartly described a feature as a work that not only wastes valuable news space, but is generally written by relatives of the publisher. In my case, the feature was a column called "Patio Puns," which meant that most of it was composed on some girl's patio and contained no puns of any kind. I was never given a by-line for this feature, but my flair for humor was plainly evident, and if there was any doubt about the anonymous authorship I soon spread the word around. I invented, or cribbed, snappy sayings and clever jokes, such as this:

> Student in college cafeteria: Waiter, I can't eat this stuff. Call the manager!
> Waiter: No use. He won't eat it either.

Needless to say, there was eventually a new columnist on *The Aztec* and, despite implications to the contrary by some of my current critics, I did not save up my leftover jokes for my coming television career.

From time to time, I wrote little mystery stories in which the mystery was how they got printed. There was one which began: "A dank, sinister, ominous blackness hung thickly over the great, blank-windowed home, and there was a shrill, hysterical scream like the cry of a lost soul." The crying sound probably came from my English teacher, Professor Florence Smith. Once, in a moment of exasperation, she suggested that some chilly night I get a nice little fire going and throw my thesaurus into it. "You are a Noah's Ark writer," she said. "Your adjectives come in two by two."

At Professor Smith's urging, I entered a college essay contest sponsored by the Phi Beta Kappa Alumni Association of Southern California. I wrote a scholarly discourse called "The Great American Ear"—it was a supercritical analysis of radio broadcasting—and to Professor Smith's happy surprise, to say nothing of my own, I came in third.

The prize was a book order worth ten dollars. I turned in a list of the books I wanted, and if I may say so, not even the late Professor Einstein could have chosen a more imposing selection of egghead titles, such as *Inner Medullary Analysis of the Sciadophycus Stellatus.* There was great rejoicing around the English department, not only because little San Diego State wound up third against such giants as the University of Southern California, but because Linkletter apparently hungered for monumental literary works.

So they scouted around for some time chasing down the rare books I wanted, and finally got them. I took the volumes to a bookstore in downtown San Diego—which I had already visited to determine what books would bring the most money—and sold them. When the school authorities sorrowfully learned that the bookstore had made up my list and that I had then sold my prize down the river, they looked on me as a sort of Ponzi who had betrayed everybody from Socrates to Aldous Huxley, and they tried to withdraw my award. The money, thank heavens, had already been spent, and not on intellectual pursuits.

Professor Smith was undoubtedly wounded by my financial deception, but she did not lose faith. She wanted me to try for a Rhodes Scholarship, and she hoped I would turn into a fine writer.

Years later, when I made a sentimental return visit to the campus, I made a point of seeing her before I talked to anyone else. I told her about my many successful radio shows, and some of the spectacular pageants I had written for the Dallas and San Francisco world's fairs. I told her I was then making one hundred thousand dollars a year and had a house with a swimming pool, and said I hoped I had justified all her hopes and dreams for me.

When I ended my proud recital, she looked at me gravely with her soft, hazel eyes. "Arthur," she said—no one else at school ever called me Arthur—"aren't you *ever* going to write something worthwhile?"

Her words are still gnawing away at me, and I admitted as

much one day to Rod Serling, the prize-winning television author. "What is worthwhile in writing, Art," he said sympathetically, "is merely a matter of semantics."

I have since consoled myself with the thought that while I have never won any prizes with my literary efforts in radio and television, even Professor Smith might concede that I have at least contributed some gay nonsense to a world that desperately needs laughter, and along the way I have cheered up millions of sick, worried or lonely people. And if not, you can be sure I'll hear from my sponsors first thing in the morning.

6. Take Back Your Waldorf Salad

Silent from the time of his birth and apparently unable to talk, a six-year-old boy suddenly said at breakfast one morning: "Hey, Mom, the toast is burnt."

His astonished mother cried out happily: "Jimmie! You talked! How come you never talked before?"

"Well," Jimmie said, "up to now everything's been okay."

MY FIRST THREE years at San Diego State were more than okay, and few people heard any complaints from me, even though there were times when I felt as though I had been sentenced to a life of endless study and work.

I had heard the fiction—and this is still a deathless premise—that college is a time of fulfillment, a cherished period of youth when the future is being molded, and when you make lasting friendships. There are charming little romances, some sweet, some sad, set against a background of picnics at the beach, hand-in-hand strolls along oak-lined campus walks, dances in the moonlight. You may not get through Calculus and Advanced Spanish, but you learn what a girl really means when she peers deep into your eyes and says: "Please don't."

I don't mean to suggest that I was not getting an education. I was, indeed.

There was the time, for instance, when I put the following ad in the college paper:

> WANTED—By 6'1" blond, blue-eyed basketball-play-ing student, a girl. 17 to 20, height 5'3", attractive, good figure, superlative dancer, brown hair and dark eyes. There is opportunity for advancement for the right party. Box 711

The ratio of women to men being what it is, especially in college, I got a number of provocative replies, and by a process of elimination, I arranged a date with one of the girls. She was a pert little beauty majoring in art, and she looked as though she might major in Art Linkletter. We went to the movies, I think, and at the end of a thoroughly innocent evening she said: "Know why I answered your letter? I'm interested in your body."

"My w-h-a-a-t?" I gasped.

"Your body," she said. "I mean—I want to paint you."

"Oh . . ." I said.

It turned out that she was a student in a life class sponsored by the City of San Diego, with outdoor sessions in a secluded corner of Balboa Park. A little investigation showed that models for this class were paid a dollar an hour, and I appeared for work looking like Hercules—I thought. The gorgeous lass was there, and it was an odd feeling, to say the least, to be standing up there in front of her, in the glaring daylight, completely naked except for a sort of homemade G-string.

So I'm watching this beautiful girl—she had soft red hair flowing down over her shoulders—and she's watching me. I rippled my muscles and expanded my chest and let her have the full profile. When the period ended, I put on a robe and walked up to her. She had a canvas three feet long and two feet wide, and she cried: "It's the best I've ever done!" She gave me a rapturous gaze, and I could see myself hanging in the Louvre, or in one of Vic Tanny's salons, though of course he wasn't around yet.

Then I looked, and that was the end of my interest in her, in modeling and in fine art in general. She had painted my right hand. Four fingers and a thumb, and nothing else. If any of my jaundiced contemporaries in Hollywood say: "Linkletter will do anything for a fast buck," they're absolutely right. I did.

During the summers, when the campus was deserted and there were no jobs at all, I worked as a lifeguard.

One season I was assigned to a crude auxiliary swimming pool out in Mission Valley. Construction crews working on dams and other projects had bulldozed enormous pits from the sand hills and these holes, filled with water, were converted into muddy but fairly satisfactory extra pools in the city recreation system.

The murky water frothed and boiled with hundreds of boys all summer long. There was never an evening that some of them didn't go home without leaving a shirt or sweater or one shoe—as small boys will—in the locker rooms. Many others would go on to the movies or a sandlot ball game without letting their mothers know. Therefore, at sundown I had the grim responsibility—with prods from frantic parents—of swimming around under water, feeling beneath floating rafts and exploring the bottom for little bodies. Luckily there were no drownings and my safety record was perfect.

Then, toward the end of the season, I was ready to go home one evening when a boy came out of nowhere near the shallow end of the pool and dove head-first over a bush into two feet of water. I saw him crumple, and when I reached him, after diving in fully clothed, he was drifting face down.

I carried him to the bank, used artificial respiration, and was relieved to see him coming around.

"Son," I said, "you know you're not supposed to dive in that end of the pool."

"My arms hurt," he said. "Fix my arms."

I looked at his arms, and they were limp. I carried him to my car, and we drove directly downtown to his family doctor —as I had been instructed to do in such emergencies. The physician helped me lift the boy to a table, and some time later he came into the waiting room shaking his head.

"How is he, Doc?" I asked.

"Not so good," the doctor said. "He's got a broken back."

The boy died four days later, and for months afterward I was torn with guilt. I shouldn't have moved him. I should have had the doctor come to the pool. I could have cut my tongue out for scolding him. It was my first meeting with death, and it depressed me for a long time. I never went back to that pool again.

The following summer I was engaged as lifeguard at Del Mar on the Pacific Ocean, an exclusive stretch of beach which was then the summer gathering place of wealthy families from Pasadena. A beach in summertime is a natural hunting ground for predatory young men, and the sands abounded with young and tender game. I was nineteen years old, about to be a senior at San Diego State, and a season on the college swimming team had given me unusually fine training for the summer job. The ocean water was cool and green, and the surf sighed gently as it caressed the slim, tanned legs of the sirens along the beach. "Keep your eyes open," my employers warned. "There's always some know-it-all who goes out too far." I kept my eyes open, and that's how I happened to see her.

Her name was—well, it doesn't matter now—and she had the kind of a figure they never tell you about in arithmetic class. There is nothing quite as leveling as the democracy of the beach. Swim suits and trunks equalize all men and women. So does the humble ritual of the hot dog. When the sun goes down, you all gather in some malt shop, and you're in sweaters and slacks. My lady of the sand hills was the daughter of rich and prominent parents, but out there in the surf or lolling on the beach she could have been a ditch-digger's daughter for all anyone cared.

So it was a summer love.

Turbulent, consuming and forever. Until Labor Day, that is. And then she had to go home, a Cinderella in reverse, to the mansion and the spin of the debutante carousel and the last coat of varnish at the finishing school. "Come and see me, darling," she said. "I'll be waiting." I promised I would.

One evening in October, I was cleaning up my old coffee grinder of a car and found a dried gardenia under the seat. I yielded to the impulse, foolishly deciding not to telephone her in advance, and drove to Pasadena. There were massive iron gates at the entrance, and I drove up a winding road for three or four acres to the house. The car was panting like a tired horse when I got there, and little puffs of steam were popping from the radiator cap. I parked in front of this baronial mansion—it looked like something Hearst might have imported from Wales stone by stone—and rang the bell.

A butler came to the door, gave me one of those squeamish looks reserved for skid row bums, and formally announced my arrival.

I was ushered into a living room only slightly smaller than the Union Station in Los Angeles, and there I stood. The girl and her parents were playing bridge with a handsome young attorney—he was obviously a suitor—and there was gracious and costly living in every direction. The old English silver service, the Wedgwood coffee cups, oil portraits of ancestors hanging on the wall, enormous logs crackling on antique brass andirons on a hearth big enough for Bethlehem Steel.

I suddenly realized what a clod I was.

My hands felt like Ping-Pong paddles, and my eighteen-dollar suit was tight and seedy. At the beach I had been the king—here I was an awkward and inarticulate rube. They were polite, of course, but embarrassed. And when I looked at the girl's eyes—the eyes that had promised enduring love—I saw only cool amusement. The fire was out—and so was I. I mumbled something about just being in the neighborhood on my way back to school and backed out.

I now understood the meaning of an ancient locker room story about a young man who had an impassioned affair on the French Riviera with a Boston heiress, and who made the mistake of calling on her at home some months later. The butler in this case came back after announcing his name and said frostily: "Madam is sorry, sir, but wishes to inform you that in Boston, sexual intercourse is not a proper form of introduction."

I am not implying that I had any such intimacies with the lady in this case. I didn't. But the moral is inescapable. The experience taught me two things. First, the big frog from the little pond is lost when he gets into a lake. And second—don't call on anyone unless you phone first.

For this latter reason, I am now able to understand and forgive the occasional tourist who, coming from a farm community where any uninvited guest is treated to a glass of milk and homemade bread, hopefully rings the bell at my house. Hundreds of tourist maps are sold every year in Hollywood, listing the addresses of movie and television stars. The cars roll down the street, and once in awhile one parks in front of the house. The stranger, beaming with good friendship, rings the bell and says cheerily: "Is Art home? We've seen him on television back home in Nebraska and just wanted to say hello."

Most of the time I am out, of course, but as a rule I don't like to have visitors coming around unannounced. I would be happy to meet the family from Nebraska at the studio, but when people come to my house for an informal visit, I know everything will end up a bit on the awkward side—as it did when I went to Pasadena long years ago.

As an afterthought, there are also tourist sightseeing busses in our neighborhood every day. They pause at the curb for a moment, and through my window I can see people bang away with their cameras and make notes as the guide gives his spiel. I wish I knew what he was saying about us. I am sure his patter is more exciting and glamorous than we are, but at least he's saying something. When the guides no longer bring the bus to our house, and when people stop staring and pointing and taking pictures, then I will know I need either a new show or a new press agent. Or both.

ii

In September, 1933, just before classes began at San Diego State, I saw a little notice posted on the student bulletin board about a job that offered room and board and a small salary in exchange for part-time housework. I drove out to case the neighborhood, and when I saw the house I knew I had to live there.

The house crowned the brow of a hill at the end of Walnut Street, and there was a carpet of lawn and garden which stretched to the edge of a cliff. Two hundred feet below was the stippled mirror of San Diego Bay, and the water tumbled gently against the shore. The estate suggested money and luxuries I had never known, and I jumped with joy when, after an exploratory interview, I got the job.

There was a mutual understanding—if I can call it that—about my place in this house.

It was owned by an elderly couple named Wilson, and Mrs. Wilson had a brother who was living with them. They had made their money in mining, and by most standards were considered wealthy, with chauffeur-driven cars and servants to run the house.

My salary was fifteen dollars a month. I had a very pleasant, comfortable room and it was agreed that they would give me breakfast and dinner. In exchange, I was to sweep and dust some of the rooms, mow the lawn, cut firewood and perform any other little necessary chores. I also had to get up early, cook three breakfasts and deliver them on silver trays to their bedrooms.

In the evening I worked alongside the family cook in the kitchen, fixing salads and desserts. At exactly seven-thirty I put on a white coat and served dinner in an enormous dining room overlooking the bay. I fixed my own dinner afterwards, and then drove back to the campus for basketball practice— by this time I was on the varsity team—and came back to do my homework.

I worked for the Wilsons almost a year. It was a year of excitement, discovery and incredibly hard work, and it brought the turning point in my life, the moment when I knew exactly where I was going.

During that nine or ten months at the Wilsons', I probably averaged less than six hours' sleep a night, but I was young and strong, and I could take it. My scrapbook shows—not that I could forget it—that I scored thirty-two points in two games against LaVerne College that season, a Conference record that stood up until the advent of one-hand shot wizards and a new concept of offensive play. San Diego State won the Conference title in the spring of 1933, and I had the honor of being named All-Conference Center.

Perhaps Mrs. Wilson should be credited with an assist.

That winter, when I had to play basketball every weekend, it took considerable conniving and soft-soaping to get time off. I offered to perform extra little jobs on Saturday morning, and among other things Mrs. Wilson asked me to gather up all the pillows in the house, and fluff them up out in the fresh air.

I kept my second-story room window open, and many a Saturday morning I shook and punched a dozen pillows. Then, using a two-hand arching shot—one of my best—I lofted them through the window into my room. I was just getting the range one morning when a shot went awry just as Mrs. Wilson poked her head through her own window to investigate the little plopping sounds she was hearing. The pillow sailed into her room and I was red-faced and embarrassed when, a moment later, she came out of the house, as regal and unruffled as the Queen Mother of England.

"Arthur," she said quietly—and if I hadn't felt quite so silly I might have detected a twinkle in her eye, "I don't think this is very good for the pillows, and I would prefer that you carry them back into the house instead of throwing them."

"Yes, Ma'am," I said.

"And what's worse," she said, walking away, "you missed."

I have never had the time nor inclination to read Emily Post's erudite composition on etiquette, but as I look back now it seems to me that I got the whole course on good manners from Mrs. Wilson. She sailed into the butler's pantry one evening, for instance, just as I was dousing a choice steak with ketchup.

"Arthur!" she said sternly. "Nice pople don't put ketchup on a steak of this quality. If you feel you cannot get along without ketchup, I will be happy to order hamburger for you."

In recent years, I have cheated a few times in restaurants where the steaks are not quite what they were at the Wilson house. Mrs. Wilson has been dead for some years now, but I can almost see her peering over my shoulder and saying: "Arthur! How could you?"

She taught me many things for which I am grateful—little niceties of manner which were not on the curriculum at San Diego State or at the Y. She rarely scolded, but when she made a point of something in her restrained, aristocratic way, I never forgot it. When I later had children of my own, and wanted them to learn the simple courtesies, my mind was filled with the echoes of that memorable year on the Walnut Street hill. *Arthur, your elbows are on the table. Arthur, one never cuts lettuce with a knife. Arthur, when you sneeze, please cover it with a handkerchief. Arthur, did you write a thank-you note to the Smiths for that sweater?* I often wish, when I see how much discourtesy there is in the world, that there could be a Mrs. Wilson for every boy.

iii

I was having lunch somewhere recently with my friend, Bob Cummings, and as we were examining the menu he exclaimed: "Ah—Waldorf salad! One of God's great gifts to the gourmet."

"Give it back," I said.

I had to explain to Bob—as I have to many other show business friends—that my dislike for this popular dish goes back to my college days when, along with my work at the Wilson home and other odd jobs, I also toiled in the San Diego State cafeteria. I reported for work at noon, as did most of the other athletes, and usually got out in time for a one-thirty class.

One of my assignments was to make the Waldorf salads, and there must be hundreds of men and women alive today whose innards are still carrying around bits of walnut shells I accidentally put into the salads. The statistics would show that I chopped up eight or ten tons of celery, and used up the apples from all the orchards between San Diego and Walla Walla, Washington. My reflexes are so conditioned that the mere mention of the word Waldorf immediately brings on grating noises in my ears—the clatter of dishes, the hiss from the steam table, the drone of voices in the crowded cafeteria. And in my mind there is a picture of an assembly line of Waldorf salads, marching along the counter and on out the window to infinity.

I also served the coffee—gallons of it—and it is no coincidence that I drink almost no coffee today.

Some of my skeptical friends in Hollywood often make fun of what they call my Horatio Alger days, and press me into service as a waiter at their parties. The greatest performance I ever gave was at the home of Alice and Charlie Correll—he is the Andy of Amos & Andy—when I carried in six cups and saucers stacked on one arm. There was only one little casualty. Alice saw me balancing her beautiful and expensive china, and had to be steadied with smelling salts.

The cafeteria operation at school was supervised by a man named Babe Morrison, and as a businessman he was naturally anxious to show a profit.

Babe was a trusting man, and he managed the cafeteria with the assumption that all the athletes who worked there would pay for their lunch. I am not so sure about the others, but when I was there a certain amount of food was permanently detoured somewhere between the steam table and the cashier's desk. Many of us were stationed right behind the steam table, and it is not surprising that when the time came for us to shed our aprons and buy our lunch, none of us was very hungry. If Babe Morrison was tearing his hair when the books consistently showed a loss—and I know he was—this confession will explain everything. In my two years at the cafeteria I did not pay for a single lunch. Babe later left San Diego State and opened his own business in San Diego. It would be superfluous to add that it has not the remotest connection with any restaurant.

iv

Remembering my work and study schedule at school—to say nothing of my athletic program—I don't see how I had time for any fun or social activities. But I did.

I was a dance addict, and I didn't need any coaxing from an Arthur Murray to start my feet moving around wherever and whenever girls and music were available. I never missed a college dance, and when there was a prom or some similar affair at San Diego High, I was qualified to be there—I told myself— as an interested alumnus. Street dances under the moonlight— on asphalt sprinkled with corn meal—were especially alluring.

Even now—at an age when the leg muscles are not as elastic as they once were—I am a pushover for a big band and soft lights, and can easily outwhirl any of my creaking friends in show business. I said as much on a recent House Party show as I picked out a pretty young dance teacher for an interview, and she implied that I needed a valve job and had two left feet.

I called over to our studio band leader, Muzzy Marcellino, and said: "Hey, Muzz—let's have a little spinning music."

I pulled the skeptical girl out of the audience, took her down on the floor and gave her thirty pivots so fast that we had a fall-out of bobby pins, combs, bracelets and other flying objects in every direction. My nationwide audience—I am told—was as incredulous as the Catskill villagers when Rip Van Winkle came down out of the hills under his own power.

What my audience didn't know was that I am one of the few entertainers alive who danced his way—perhaps stumbled is the word—into a wife and five other tax deductions, or children as they are more popularly known.

I went to a dance one Saturday evening at the Hotel Del Coronado in San Diego—there is no more enchanting seaside setting for lovers, young or old—and during a tag dance, I found myself with a gorgeous creature who was a new face to me. We started pivoting, but I thought she was being a little clumsy about it, and I said: "If we're going to do this well, you'll have to wrap your legs around mine a lot closer than they are."

She stopped dead in the middle of the floor and gave me a sub-zero look that would have frozen Admiral Byrd. "Well . . . !" she said, exhaling explosively, "I've never been talked to like that before, and you can bet it's the last time. What's more, I think you're the most conceited fellow I've ever known."

She did some fast broken-field running to get off the floor, and I did not see her again that night. Six months later—by this time I was a senior at college—I was still showing up at every dance within a twenty-mile radius. I was president of the Associated Men Students, and I was captain of the basketball team. I could have become involved in all sorts of nonessential activities on the campus—such as the Chess Club, the Stamp

Society and the Association for the Improvement of Freshman Girls. But deflation had not set in yet, and I was a big wheel on the campus. The dances had a certain status, and all the wheels went.

One winter evening my fraternity, Tau Delta Chi, held its annual dance at the La Jolla Beach and Yacht Club, and when I got there I saw one of the brothers, Allen Flavin, gliding around the floor with the bewitching little minx who had given me the brush at the Del Coronado the preceding spring. I nudged Flavin during an intermission and asked him to introduce me.

"No," he said. "Go 'way."

"Why not?" I asked. "You're my pal."

"Not any more, boy," he said. "Every time I get a new girl you muscle in, and then I have to start all over."

Flavin was absolutely right, but there was no trade-in that night. The girl didn't want to dance with me—as Flavin let me know later on—and at the fraternity ball the big wheel turned out to be just a spare. But it didn't take long to learn that her name was Lois Foerster, that she was the daughter of Mr. and Mrs. Charles J. Foerster of San Diego, and that she was guarded at home like the Hope diamond. Lois was wearing a black sequin jacket that evening—how could I ever forget it—and she was wearing her hair in bangs. I told myself that something would have to be done about the bangs.

The next day I phoned her at home and asked for a date.

"But I don't even know you," she said. "And my mother doesn't know you, and I don't think she'd like you. You'll have to talk to her."

"Put your sweet little mother on the phone," I said impudently. And right then and there I began my ad-lib selling career with a commercial that today would sell a boxcar of cornflakes.

Mrs. Foerster came to the phone and said in her soft cool voice: "I don't know you, Mr. Linkletter. Lois does not go out with strange boys."

"Mrs. Foerster," I began—and this turned out to be the best soft-sell pitch of my life, "I know you don't know me. But you do know your daughter, and any mother who has brought up a girl the way you've brought up Lois can trust her with anyone, stranger or not."

I have often wondered why Mrs. Foerster fell for that verbal sleight of hand. I never asked her. Perhaps she wasn't tricked at all. Some mothers will do anything to get rid of ——. Well, anyway, she asked me to come to the house. I got in the jaloppy and went right out. Mrs. Foerster answered the doorbell, and I knew instantly that I had a friend at court. She was the gentle, warm-hearted kind of woman you see symbolized in the Mother's Day posters, and I had only been in the house two or three minutes, nervously and stiffly perched on the rim of a sofa, when she offered me cookies and milk.

So we started our companionship in the kitchen, where the social life begins in most American homes, and Lois joined us there.

As I recall the situation, I was so hypnotized by this girl—and up to that time I had considered myself fairly sophisticated and invulnerable—that during an important Conference game the following weekend, I put my jersey on backwards and missed four easy lay-up shots. I would have married her right then except for a few minor obstacles. I had no job nor promising future, and at that point she wouldn't have married me anyway.

The happy little world of the Foersters—and they gave me a passport to come and go as I pleased—was a transition with such emotional impacts that for awhile it was difficult to readjust. With the Linkletters, I had been stifled by narrow boundaries and Biblical strait jackets. Leaving home for a year as a nomad on the open road, I had seen the life in jungles and gutters. With Denver Fox and his brothers the daily routine was a boisterous shambles, and with the Samuels, life had a happy gypsy quality. At the Wilsons I saw wealth with a Dickensonian cloak.

But here was the normal American family with a charm and security and unity I had never known.

Charles Foerster was a successful druggist who owned and operated a pharmacy of his own on Fifth Street in downtown San Diego. He was a hunter and fisherman, and the kind of man every young fellow hopes to get for a father-in-law. His pretty daughters, Lois and Jacqueline, were taught the rules and codes of our times, and were expected to honor them without sacrificing their own rights and thoughts. In short, this was a solid family—with no false images or distorted perspective. I was crazy about them all.

During my last year at San Diego State, Lois was a freshman on the same campus.

I took her home on the slightest excuse, of course, and I was the man who came to dinner. Compared to the assembly-line chow at the college cafeteria, Peg Foerster's cooking was the work of Escoffier himself, and if all the pot roasts I ate there were laid end to end, they'd reach around my waistline because that's where they went.

At some point during our courtship, or perhaps it was before I met Lois (there is an understandable confusion when I try to reconstruct these dizzying events), my friend John Crofton and I wrote the music and lyrics for the annual college "Aztec Follies." The musical was called "Pressure"—I think we whimsically gave it that title because the pressure was on to raise money for the student loan fund—and it drew a full house.

In any case, my first adventure in show business was sufficiently impressive that I was asked to organize the "Follies" a second time. In my scrapbook, though, I see a small item from the college paper which reads: "Art Linkletter resigned from his position as Production Manager for the 'Aztec Follies' due to the pressure of outside business." The outside business, no doubt, was Miss Lois Foerster.

One noon I was handing out Waldorf salads—and glad to get rid of them—when I was called to the phone in the cafeteria. Over the clatter of breaking saucers and glasses I heard a voice saying: "This is Lincoln Dellar, the manager at Radio Station KGB. I wonder if you'd come down and talk to me about a part-time job as a radio announcer?"

"Yes, *sir!*" I gulped.

Later I learned that Professor Harry Steinmetz, who was my psychology teacher, had been impressed with my work as an assistant in his class, and he knew that Dellar had been looking for a college student to help out around the studio. I got the job, and the moment I had that first microphone in my hand, I thought I would never want to do anything else.

So between Lois and Radio KGB, I was spinning like a roulette wheel, and all the right numbers were coming up. More or less, that is. My first outside broadcasting job was at the Mission Beach Ballroom in San Diego, and I was assigned to do the announcing for the opening performance of Freddy Martin and his orchestra. Freddy Martin was a very big name indeed, and I took Lois along to let her see what an important young man I was. We walked up to the bandstand to meet Freddy, and I was holding Lois' hand.

"I want you to meet Miss ———" I began.

My mind suddenly stripped a gear, and I simply could not remember Lois' name. Freddy gave me a quizzical look as I struggled with this blackout, and Lois, reddening, grimly kept silent.

"Well . . ." I said lamely, "this is Miss somebody. I just picked her up tonight."

Lois gasped, gave me a five-thousand volt shot with her eyes, and stormed out. I never did tell Freddy Martin that Lois and I were then engaged, and if he reads this now he will know why my radio debut was wrecked almost before my career began. As for Lois—well, she never let me forget it, and, I imagine, when she wants to cut me down a few rungs she quietly tells our five children what an ungallant young idiot I was.

7. Adventures of a Newlywed

One evening many years ago, I passed my son Jack's bedroom and paused for a moment as he said his bedtime prayers. And this is what I heard: "Thank you, God. Amen. Listen in again tomorrow night. Same time, same station, for another in this series."

My first impulse was to step into the room, scold him a little and explain that perhaps God was tuned into the Linkletter house, but that He was considerably different from a radio audience and should be treated with more dignity. But I didn't. I quietly shut the door and went downstairs.

I realized that little Jack was not only imitating me, which was natural, but that since his birth he had heard little else around the house but the jargon and shoptalk of my business. Jack is twenty-three now and, I am proud to say, has created and starred in his own television show. He has learned all that I could teach him—and more—but I suspect he is saying his prayers quite differently now.

BROADCASTING HAS DOMINATED my life, as my family knows, and I have been living it every minute, day and night, since my college days.

I was still working part-time at Station KGB in San Diego

when graduation time came around in June, 1934. I stood at the crossroads, as many another senior has done, and faced the challenge of the future. There were two choices for me then. I had majored in English, had always loved working with words and for a while had considered a teaching career with its lifetime security.

The first teaching position offered would have paid $120 a month, but KGB was already paying me $125 as an announcer, and that five dollars became the big difference. In that depression period, the extra five dollars, stretched a little, might pay the gas bill if two people were cooking up meals instead of one. And this was exactly what I had in mind for Miss Lois Foerster.

In the give and take of love, or so the experts say, the best strategy is a backcourt defensive position. I had the positive feeling that Lois wasn't quite sold on me yet, and so I retreated.

"Look, honey," I said one day, "why don't you go away for a year?"

"Go away?" she said, puzzled. "Where? Why?"

"Well," I said, "you've been wanting to go on to a second year of college, and it might be interesting to pick one out of state."

"Oh . . ." she said. "I see."

I knew very well that Lois had had no intention of going anywhere. But she was always sensitive and independent, and the mere intimation that I could live without her was enough to put her in flight. She registered as a sophomore at the University of Arizona in Tucson, and I was not to see her again, except for a few brief hours during the holidays, until the following year. I don't know what the gossips were saying— this kind of news unfortunately travels faster than a Winchell stock market tip—but presently I was elected to an alumni membership in the San Diego State Bachelors' Club. I went to all the meetings and got my copy of the regular club bulletin which, as I recall, was a list of interesting new phone numbers.

It was a sad fact of my life at that time that I had a handsome diploma certifying that I was a Bachelor of Arts but I couldn't cash it at the supermarket. I had saved no money at all, and this acute shortage was made evident one day when I had a mishap on the highway. I was dawdling along San Diego Boulevard and enjoying the scenic beauty of a wooded canyon just below the road. As I rounded a curve I saw a girl I knew emerging from the trees, followed by a young man whose face I couldn't see. I have always had a scientific interest in the flora and fauna of the region and I wondered what they had found in the woods that made them so flushed with excitement.

I craned my neck out the window for another look and— crunch—I smacked into a shiny limousine. I recognized it as the chauffeur-driven car of the Marston family, a rich and influential San Diego clan, and I imagined high-priced lawyers closing in on me and I could hear the judge putting me away for five years. I scrambled out of my badly dented clunk, rushed across the road and yelled at the chauffeur: "Why don't you watch where you're going?!"

The chauffeur was so startled that he was struck dumb for a moment. "Well . . ." he said lamely, "I was doing my best, but you kept coming farther and farther over on my side of the road. Look at your tire marks on the pavement!"

"It certainly wasn't my fault," I said belligerently, overlooking the damaging evidence. "I'm sure the Marstons will be glad to get my car fixed."

I am ashamed to say that eventually the Marstons not only footed the bill for the wrinkles on their limousine, but paid for my repairs, too. I am grateful that they did because there was no question about the fact that I was responsible for the crash, and I didn't have a dime. I would have been forced to walk to the Foerster home for the pot roast and the latest news about Lois. The news was not always good.

While I was slaving away at KGB and thinking that the single life was not for me, Lois was making long gains with the captain of the University of Arizona football team. I was doing a little quarterbacking myself, of course, but there was nothing at stake, and my passes were always incomplete. The truth is, I was lonely without Lois, and my life would have been aimless and disconnected without the challenge of the job at KGB. I was getting a baptism in the exciting but often disastrous art of ad libbing.

ii

In television today I am generally considered to be primarily an ad-lib man. That is, I usually work without a typed script. Over the years, in countless newspaper and magazine interviews, I have been asked about the art of ad libbing, and whether it really exists in the mass-production entertainment we have today. The term is an abbreviation, of course, for the Latin phrase Ad Libitum, which means "as one pleases" or, "as one wishes." To me the true ad lib is a remark you pull out of the air to fit a situation of the moment, and if it gets a laugh you're lucky.

I wish my mind could grind out the quips as easily as Bob Hope, Milton Berle or Groucho Marx. It is an education for me—or any performer—to be with my friend Groucho, for instance, but I have long since stopped trying to talk sense with him.

He once went to a performance by a clever magician who

could thread needles, half a dozen at a time, with his tongue or his teeth, inside his mouth. He began the act by placing the unthreaded needles on his tongue alongside pieces of thread, opening his mouth and asking the audience: "What do you see?"

Groucho snapped loudly: "Cavities."

Another time my partner, John Guedel, and I were sitting around the office with Groucho—our company packages the Groucho Marx Show—and we were chatting about business conditions. Guedel said glumly: "Prices are too darn high."

"Why don't the Prices move down to the third floor?" Groucho said. "The view isn't as good but they won't get dizzy."

Guedel ignored the remark, but Groucho was off and running. "I knew some Prices in Pocatello," he said. "Sam and Evelyn Price. Sam had a poodle and a beautiful wife. She had fleas. The dog, I mean. Or maybe they all had 'em—"

"Groucho, please!" Guedel interrupted.

"The whole family started from scratch," Grouch droned on. "Somebody was always putting the bite on them."

Guedel shrugged helplessly.

"My, my," Groucho said, "they were certainly loused up."

We managed to cut him off at that point, but he could have gone on indefinitely. I have tried this word-extension technique myself, but I can't compete with the sort of weird writhings inside the Marx brain. As I look back on my apprentice days, it seems to me that my first hesitant ad libs often backfired, as more than one sponsor complained. The KGB files will show— or maybe they've already burned them in disgust—that Linkletter probably induced more apoplexy around the station than any announcer before or since.

One of my first assignments at KGB was to read commercials for a used-car dealer, but the message seemed uninspired. One day I threw away the typed page and said: "Folks, the Lemon Used Car Lot has something you've been waiting for. A big sedan with four new tires, reconditioned engine, new paint. Hurry down and take a good look because *here's one car that won't last long*." Mr. Lemon—and that's not his real name, of course—was on the phone immediately, screaming: "And you can tell Linkletter that for my money he's one *announcer* who won't last long."

Covering a rodeo, I tried to inject some excitement into the broadcast by crying: "Yes, folks, here is the biggest horse I've ever seen. It must weigh two or three tons!" The repercussions from this innocent remark—after all, I had never weighed a horse—were frightening. I got denunciatory mail from horse owners, jockeys, stable boys, trainers and movie cowboys. They all suggested, none too delicately, that an announcer who doesn't know that most horses weigh only about half a ton has no business talking about them to the public. I even had a telegram from the late Bob "Believe It or Not" Ripley, offering me five hundred dollars for a photograph of a three-ton horse, dead or alive.

Another time, confronted by a drunken heckler, I sidestepped his pawing until the program ended, and then I let him have it. "You so-and-so!" I said angrily, "if you're not out of here in two minutes I'm going to knock your damned head off!" The microphone was still open, alas, and my cussing rattled the loudspeakers in hundreds of homes.

There was a period when I experimented with sound effects —this job belonged to the technicians, but I thought I could do it, too—and there came a challenging assignment to recreate the Battle of the Marne. It was a hair-raising theme, to say the least, and was to end with a thunderous boom from a cannon.

I had decided I could get the proper effect by firing a double-barreled shotgun into an empty beer barrel. I pulled the triggers right on cue, and the Battle of the Marne was over. So was my career as a sound effects man. The show's sponsor, who was sitting in an adjoining booth, had twenty-five feet of plate glass in his lap, and the pieces of the bursting beer barrel were impaled on all four walls. The microphone looked like a burned omelet, and the transmitter was dead. The blast could have killed us all, but luckily no one was hurt. No one except the bookkeepers, that is, for that sponsor never came back.

These errors—and there were many others—made me a natural target for the jokers on the station staff. I am familiar with fraternity hazing, and I once got the works from my fellow crew members on the S. S. "American Legion" when I crossed the Equator on my bumming trip, but these initiations were elemental compared to the indoctrination I got at KGB.

They touched matches to my script when I was reading stock quotations or dropped squirming cats on my head during a newscast. They tickled me with feathers, or deftly removed my pants and left me standing there in my shorts. And they gave me the mixed-script treatment, a classic radio gag, which has the same effect as a mickey. I was on the air with a spot news broadcast about a marine disaster—and this is how it went:

> "Bulletin! At last report the burning ship was located 28 miles east of Hawaii. The ship's captain told the Coast Guard by radio that all he could do was—"

I flipped to the second page and continued at a breathless pace:

> "—to beat the egg whites thoroughly before adding cream."

Just below this line, printed in pencil, was this little footnote: "And now where in hell are you, Bud?" Oh, they were cards, all right. The culprits were virtually rolling on the floor in the control booth, and I must have lost fifteen seconds, an eternity in terms of a dead mike, before I went on to the third page and finished the newscast.

Now, I admit I was irritated and momentarily thrown by the mixed-script bit, but in retrospect I can see that it was a form of training. I not only learned to anticipate a crisis now and then, but I also realized that most scripts are a form of confinement. In short, there was an exhilarating freedom about an ad-lib show, and if there were going to be errors—or fluffs, as we call them—at least they would be my own. I have never worked any other way since.

iii

In the spring of 1935, while Rome was burning in Tucson— by this time it was Lois and the captain of the baseball team—I was fiddling with the dials and buttons at KGB and learning the trade.

About that time, I met a big, drawling, easy-going reformed Colorado cowhand named Clyde Vandeburg. "Jughead"—as some of us called him because he was all ears and usually laughing—had moved to San Diego to join the Chamber of Commerce staff, and had just been appointed promotion director for the San Diego International Exposition. This was a miniature world's fair in San Diego's Balboa Park, with an opening date set for May 29. The theme was "Not the end of an era of progress, but the beckoning future, the beginning of a cycle of larger advancement and human accomplishment." It could have been written for me.

I was not only a staff announcer at KGB, but was also the station publicity director, and I was shamelessly spreading the name of Linkletter around. I got in all the photographs of studio dance bands, for instance, and in one of these pictures I was holding a tuba. In another I was standing beside a bull fiddle. These instruments and I were total strangers, but the pictures gave the impression that I had musical talent, too, and that consequently our music programs were on a slightly higher level than those of rival stations. This program of self-promotion was so effective that when I gave a learned address at the San Diego Rotary Club, the newspaper reports identified the speaker as Arthur Ledbetter.

Anyway, Vandeburg said without preliminaries one day: "Art, why don't you get a leave from the station job and join me at the fair?"

"Van," I said, "the fair's only going to run a few months. My job here is secure, and there's no future at all with you. So I'll do it."

It was probably one of the most important career decisions I ever made, for it took me out of the steady, solid little world of San Diego for a while, and eventually led me along a twisting, bumpy road to the big time in radio and television. There were days at the fair when the going was very rough indeed, and among my souvenirs is a treasured letter from Van in which he wrote:

> "Art—Thanks for the excellent job on the Ford Bowl show tonight. Don't forget that I'm in your corner all the time, and if I seem a bit harsh at times you must realize that I'm aiming more at our organization than at you as an individual. I like you a lot. I think you are going places, and I will be standing by to give you a lift when needed."

Clyde Vandeburg and I are still business associates and when he came out from New York on a recent visit I reminded him of his first letter. "Well, Art," he said thoughtfully, "I must have had some crazy kind of hunch. Because the fact is that when I first met you—and you were right off the campus in your big white wool sweater—I thought you were the freshest, greenest looking punk kid I ever saw. I thought you were just about old enough to run out for sandwiches."

I went to the San Diego fair with Van—where I got somebody else to get the sandwiches—and had the happy experience of meeting the sword swallowers, fan dancers, bearded ladies, snake charmers and other citizens in the strange and wonderful world of the carnival. There was a time when I felt sorry for some of these odd people, but they were always cheerful with me, and I recall one sideshow performer who said: "Don't ever worry about us. There's an old carny axiom which says: 'There are more freaks outside the tents than in.' " How right he was.

During the next twenty years, especially on the People Are Funny show, I was to meet more screwballs than Barnum ever knew, but I naturally remember the first one at the San Diego fair.

Our opening-day show had been planned to take the listener to key sections of the exposition grounds through a series of remote microphones. The late Gary Breckner, an old CBS pro, was in charge of this maze of lines and had been assigned to the switching orders from a high observation tower overlooking the entire fourteen-hundred-acre park. At the last moment, with Breckner holding his breath for the final dramatic cue, a fumbling electrician accidentally cut through the control cable with his wire cutters. Breckner was as useless as a hunter with a cap pistol, and I took over from my studio in the International Village.

I killed time with music from a rhumba band, and then cut over to the late Bill Goodwin, who was just beginning to acquire the polish that later made him one of the great announcers in radio. He was stationed in Gold Gulch, an authentic reproduction of a Wild West main street during the Gold Rush days.

"This is Bill Goodwin, folks," he said, "standing in the midst of a scene right out of the last century. Everybody's wearing a beard here, and we're being deafened by the roar of six-guns. It's the old Wild West all over again—ah, here comes one buckaroo now, twirling a pistol loaded with blanks. How about it, podner? Let's see how fast you can draw."

The buckaroo, feeling the two or three belts of firewater he had lapped up before the show started, rode up to Goodwin's mike, raised his equalizer and pulled the trigger. Pow! The microphone went that-a-way and Goodwin was staring at the frayed wires in his hand. For years afterward when Bill was about to go on the air with some big budget network show, I could break him up just by saying: "Let's see how fast you can draw."

iv

Lois finally came home from Tucson. I was young and I was still deeply in love, and I again began to commute to 1850 Sunset Boulevard, where the Foersters lived. Nothing had changed. She was still the girl with the bangs that needed cutting, but by now we had a wordless understanding about our future, and my financial situation had improved to the point that I could at least pay apartment rent for two.

Just before the San Diego Exposition closed, I was asked to come back to KGB as program manager. I kept the letter outlining the terms of the offer not only because it was my first shot at an executive job, but because it gave me the security I needed. There have been times now and then when some of

my investments shrank or disappeared, or when the financial
pressure of raising a family seemed intolerable, but I could
always regain my sense of humor and values by re-reading the
letter which Harry W. Witt, manager at KGB, sent me
twenty-five years ago.

> "Dear Mr. Linkletter," he wrote, "on August 15 you
> will start at KGB at a salary of $150.00 a month. If at
> the conclusion of three months your ability to get things
> done measures up to the standard you have set for your-
> self, we will arrange for a $25.00 increase in salary. We
> know you will give every ounce of effort to the job
> to be accomplished. We believe it offers opportunity for
> the right effort."

I don't recall now whether or not my programming increased the profits at KGB. Perhaps it did. I got the twenty-
five-dollar raise in mid-November, and Lois and I set our
marriage for Thanksgiving Day that same month.

Neither one of us had been regular churchgoers during our
college years and thus did not have a family minister to help
us plan the wedding. One day, just driving around together, we
passed the Grace Lutheran Church, liked its Old World charm
and went in to meet the minister, the Rev. Clarence Damschroeder. We told him we wanted a very simple ceremony
and would have just a few close friends and relatives.

On the evening of November 28, with my friend Gordie
Samuel as best man and Lois' sister Jackie as maid of honor,
we gathered in Mr. Damschroeder's study for final instruc-
tions. The Foerster family was inside the church, so was
Mother Linkletter, who had recently moved to Pomona, and
who had come to San Diego for the wedding. Suddenly there
was a rumble of voices in the garden outside, and I had the
bizarre thought that the whole University of Arizona football

team was charging in to object when the minister says: "If any man can show just cause why they may not lawfully be joined together, let him now speak or else hereafter forever hold his peace."

We peeked outside at the mob, but none of them looked like football players. They were men and women none of us recognized, and they soon filled up the church. Weeks later I learned that Bill Goodwin had announced the wedding on the entire Don Lee radio network. "If any of my listeners feel like going," Bill said, "just tell the ushers that you're Bill Goodwin's guest." Bill had a big audience, and his followers were there in platoons.

The newspapers printed our wedding picture, and described the ceremony in detail. Among other things, they reported that Lois "wore a wedding gown of eggshell velvet with a high cowl in front and a long train. Her tulle veil fell in filmy tiers from a Juliet cap of pearls. She carried cream Johanna Hills roses with stems wrapped in gold to match the gilded maidenhair fern and the gold slippers."

There were flowery descriptions of the church, the organ music and the wedding cake and how Lois had made the little bride and bridegroom figures herself. There was also a reference to the fact that "Miss Foerster had majored in Art at State College," as indeed she had. But none of the society reporters noticed that Lois came down the aisle without her customary bangs. She had cut them off—a variation of the Samson snipping —and she never wore her hair that way again. "Thus in the beginning the world was so made," said Cicero, "that certain signs come before certain events." No man could have asked for a happier omen, trifling as it may seem.

Some philosophers have said that marriage is a man's coming of age; the Bible marks it as a farewell: "Therefore shall a man leave his father and mother." As glib and garrulous as I have been all my life, I am unable to describe the sense of separation that fell like a curtain in my mind. I looked at Mother Linkletter, primly sitting next to the Foersters in the church, and she was someone I had never really known.

She had lived her whole life in a cage of her own making, and she was incredibly shy and inarticulate. She had never learned to drive a car and had never seen a motion picture because the theater was a place where sinners could indulge their evil thoughts. Neither she nor my father ever had a telephone in their home, and she was jarred and frightened by the noises of mankind—children crying, the whine of motors on the road, the ring of a telephone, any babble of voices, even in small groups. She was gentle and patient with my father's flamboyant pursuit of salvation, but it was a long-suffering patience and had made her a recluse. I knew that the short trip from Pomona had been an ordeal, not because she was old or tired and had to ride buses and streetcars, but because it meant she would have to face people.

Father Linkletter had not been able to come, as usual. He sent us a telegram from Pomona, signed Papa Linkletter. He followed it with a poignant letter to Lois, a letter that mirrored locked-up thoughts better than anything he had ever said to his adopted son.

"Thrice welcome to the Linkletter family," he wrote. "Your dear Mother No. 2 has never gotten over that visit. She still breaks out as if it were some new joy, about those lovely people. Where do *I* come in? She fell in love with the whole bunch.

"We are looking forward to a visit from you and your *husband*, Mr. Link. Or in other words our darling boy, Artie. He will always be "dear Artie" to me.

"Well, dear Lois, we are continuously praying the dear Lord to Bless You both. To honor and obey Him insures

success and carries a *promise of long life*. Psalms 91:16.
Read that Psalm, won't you dear. Bushels of love to
dear Artie and Lois.

Mama—and Old Papa"

I remembered seeing him one day shortly after I had been
appointed program manager at KGB. He had once wanted me
to be a preacher, as he was, knowing in his heart that I could
not fulfill his wish. But now he said: "You'll be able to preach
to thousands of people, Artie, more than I ever did. You can
bring them cheer and encouragement and the word of the
Lord."

I was cheerful on the radio—exuberantly so—but I was never
able to give sermons. Father did not reproach me. He merely
kept sending me little reminders to "give the Lord a plug."
After my wedding day, though he lived in nearby Pomona, he
was as far out of my life as if he had gone back to the Canadian
island where he was born.

v

At KGB, some months before Lois and I were married, we
had an announcer who, with a voice like a Tennessee coon
caller, began his morning's stint with this cry: "Hey there,
you! Get outta that bed! It's seven o'clock." One morning, an
hour or so after his program had gone off the air, there appeared a distraught and angry young man who, had he been
able to corner our raucous announcer, might have inflicted
mayhem.

We got his blood pressure down, and he finally explained his
fury. He had been married the night before, it seems, and had
started off on a honeymoon. He and his bride were sound

asleep in a motel when, from one of those automatic alarm-clock radios, came the galvanizing call: "Hey there, you! Get outta that bed!" Pavlov's reflex got an instant response. The bridegroom leaped out of bed, grabbed his pants, bounced off the nightstand and broke his wrist, and was two hundred yards down the road before he sheepishly realized the enormity of what he had done.

He went back to the motel and found his bride packing to go home to mother. Naturally he blamed our announcer, and it took some soothing talk to quiet him. Nevertheless, when our announcer went on the air the following morning this is what he said: "S-h-h-h . . . don't be alarmed . . . it's only me . . . your radio."

One of our wedding presents was a small portable radio—I assume the donor thought I might want to keep up with the business while I was on my honeymoon—but I purposely left it at home. I did not trust the jokers at KGB, and I wanted not only a quiet honeymoon, but a vacation.

We had planned to spend our first night together at the Pacific Coast Club, a private club for which we had a guest card, and we were bowling along the highway after the reception at the Foerster home, listening to a record program. The disk jockey was Sid Fuller, a KGB friend who has since become a prominent newscaster in Los Angeles. He was spinning some song—I don't remember the title—and suddenly he interrupted the music.

"Bulletin!" he cried. "Attention all innkeepers and hotel men up and down the coast! If a young couple shows up at your place and wants to register as man and wife under the names Mr. and Mrs. Art Linkletter, demand to see their marriage certificate."

I slammed on the brakes, pulled off the road and looked at Lois.

"You've got it, of course?" I said.

"No . . ." she said. "I thought you took it."

We turned our luggage inside out and made a frantic search of the car, but couldn't find it. We had dropped it running out of the church, as we learned later, and Sid Fuller had been tipped off by one of our fun-loving friends.

As it happens, the desk clerk at the Pacific Coast Club had not heard Fuller's little joke, and asked no questions at all when we signed the register. In fact, I thought he showed considerable restraint as we stood there, blushing and flicking the last grains of rice from our clothes, and he assigned us to a beautiful room on the top floor, overlooking the pounding sea.

We were half unpacked when both of us belatedly noticed the twin beds. I picked up the room phone, called the clerk and with a fumbling tongue explained to him that we . . . uh . . . that is . . . we would prefer another room.

"Double bed?" he said. "Certainly, sir."

Some minutes later there was a rap on the door, and when I opened it the bellboy was standing there with a key and a wide grin on his face. We gathered our things, trooped down the hall to another room and started all over again.

"I'm sure you'll find this an improvement," the bellboy said.

"Beat it," I said.

"Yes, *sir*," he grinned.

We stayed there that night, and drove on to Los Angeles the following afternoon. Lois' grandmother had an apartment on Vermont Street which she made available to us, and we spent four happy days there, loving, loafing and doing the town. On the way back to San Diego—I only had one week of vacation coming—we went back to the Pacific Coast Club. We had not made a reservation and our friend at the front desk shook his head dolefully as he riffled through his files.

"Frankly, Mr. Linkletter," he said, "and I hope you won't

think this is some sort of joke—the only room available right now is that one with the twin beds you didn't like."

"Great!" I said. "I'll take it."

Going home the next day we moved into a small apartment at 3587 First Avenue, unpacked our wedding presents, and faced the future better adjusted and more mature, I think, than many another couple the same age. We had been there only a week when Lois started moving the furniture around, as brides often do, and among other things there was a floor lamp which, to fit the new arrangement, needed a longer cord.

"Darling," she said sweetly, "can you fix this?"

She knew very well how to fix it herself, but I was the man of the house, of course, and she was letting me nurse the illusion that women are helpless about these things. So I took our new kitchen paring knife, cut and scraped the wires, taped them all together—the knife was never very sharp after that operation—and plugged the cord into the outlet. There was a flash of blue light and a puff of smoke—the kind that magicians use to make a pretty girl disappear on stage.

Lois vanished, too—I think she went down the back stairs. All the fuses were blown. Lois never asked me to repair anything thereafter, and I have sadly concluded that I am not the home fix-it-yourself type.

There came a day when I was invited to emcee the annual Television Academy Awards at the Statler Hotel in Los Angeles.

I was in the center of a vast stage, the orchestra was in the pit and, wandering around among the soaring pillars of a Grecian setting, were ten million dollars' worth of movie and television stars. It was a proud moment for me with forty million viewers waiting by their television sets, and my heart pounded as the network announcer said: "We now take you to Art Linkletter at the Statler Hotel."

The curtain slowly opened, and at that instant the main stage lights blew out with a spiral of blue smoke. An unidentified stage electrician, rushing to the fuse box, knocked over one of the fake Greek pillars and it toppled into the pit. The first violinist was knocked flat, and the tuba player blew a C sharp, which was not the cue note at all. I don't remember what I said as order was restored but Lois, standing in the wings, turned to Walt Disney and whispered something that has probably puzzled him ever since. "Well!" she said. "I see old fixit did it again."

8. "Mr. Linkletter— You're Fired!"

> *There was once a very successful shoe salesman on my People Are Funny show and I was naturally curious about his selling techniques.*
>
> *"How come you sell more women's shoes than anyone else?" I asked.*
>
> *"It's simple," he replied. "When a woman comes in I say: 'Let's start with the larger sizes and work down until we get that little stab of pain we're looking for.'"*

AT KGB, as an ambitious young married man, I was reversing the shoe man's system—working up to the larger sizes and getting a little stab of pain every week when I looked at my tiny pay check.

Knowing my own eagerness and ability, I could reasonably anticipate becoming an executive one day. Vice presidents don't live forever—as the late Fred Allen once philosophized in somewhat stronger language—and eventually there would be a place for me on an upper rung. But office espionage being what it is, I soon learned that the biggest station executive pay check was mere carfare compared to the money earned by the big name announcers and emcees.

At the age of twenty-three, I was the youngest program

director in the entire Don Lee Broadcasting System, which stretched from San Diego to Spokane.

Some of my San Diego friends may remember me as a sort of perpetual motion windmill—restless, spinning, burning up energy and scattering it in every direction. In my spare time I was playing basketball in the Commercial League and the Church League, and I had taken up handball, the most physically demanding, competitive individual sport of all.

I worked long hours at the station, and I began to regulate my life with a timetable—a habit to which I am still a slave. I can look at a typewritten date sheet I carry in my pocket and know exactly what I will be doing at 4:45 P.M. next Thursday, let's say, or a Thursday two months from now. I know that many people would be appalled at the thought of going through life in such a rigid framework. I'm a little appalled by it myself. But I discovered in San Diego long ago that this was the only answer for me. There are so many fascinating things in life, so many intriguing places and people, that I would never see them unless I put them on a list and check them off one by one. All we have in life is time, and I don't propose to dribble it away.

I had been program manager at KGB about seven months when Clyde Vandeburg left San Diego to become promotion director for the Texas Centennial Exposition in Dallas.

He phoned me one day and asked me to join him there as director of the fair's radio operation, and I could hardly wait. We had saved just enough money to make the trip by car, and Lois, who was always eager to explore new horizons, was happy to go. As a young housewife on a budget, of course, she wanted to know what my salary would be, and I had to tell her I didn't know.

"Didn't Van tell you how much you're going to get?" she asked in a tone of mild protest.

"I didn't ask him, honey," I said.

It is not always easy to explain these things to a bride who is naturally concerned with the arithmetic of the grocer and the landlord, but she also understood that I didn't want to be nailed down in San Diego—executive or not—for the rest of my life. We packed our bags and left home toward the end of April in 1936.

Those few months in Dallas, where I developed a lasting affection for the remarkable people of an even more remarkable empire—were a revelation to a young man who thought he knew most of the tricks of radio promotion. I found myself squirming out of awkward situations that at first offered no escape. I encountered weird people who, recognized as celebrities, still seemed just one jump ahead of white-coated men with nets. I learned to shrug off technical disasters, and I confirmed my hunch that the worst ad libbing is better than the slickest script when the floor falls out from under you.

On May 20, I was lucky to be named assistant announcer for the ceremonies which officially opened the fair.

The top man that day was Ted Husing, ace announcer in the CBS network, and I shamelessly followed him around all day, watching every move he made, taking mental notes on what he said and how he said it. My first impression of Husing was a disappointment. We discussed details of the network broadcast, and I had the feeling that his conversation was careless and profane. Frankly, I wondered how this happy-go-lucky man had made such a name for himself.

The show was to open with a parade and a pageant at the Cotton Bowl, with the United States Marine Band as a musical herald.

Outside the grounds, as the line of traffic thickened and clotted, frantic officials saw the Marine Band being blocked off. In the emergency, they pulled the musicians off the main thoroughfare and directed them down a side street on a detour that would lead to a rear exit. Unfortunately they picked the wrong street. Flags flying and drums beating, the band disappeared from view and wound up far in the suburbs to the surprised delight of homeowners who hadn't seen a parade in years.

In this crisis Husing underwent a magic transformation. Here was the master ad libber at work. Microphone in hand, he began spraying the air with excitement. It was like painting a scene with bullets, and every word drilled into your ears and made your head ring.

Husing was superb, but it was many years before I got around to telling him how much he had taught me that day. Nearly blind and partly paralyzed after a brain tumor operation, he was led on stage during a recent House Party program, and it was with great personal pride that I presented him with a national YMCA award for his work in sports.

The Dallas adventure was twenty-five years ago, and the details of my 1,040 broadcasts there have naturally faded considerably. But there are a few frames in the film which are still vividly clear.

During one network show broadcast from the Midway zone, I was collaring married men and asking them to talk about their children. I stopped one likely prospect and asked how many children he had.

"There's at least nine," he said.

Perhaps I should have been warned by the defiant look in his eyes. But I was still learning in those days and I didn't shut him off. "My, my," I said, "life must be pretty hectic around your house."

"I don't have a house," he said. "I'm a bachelor."

"Now just a min—" I snapped.

"I'm a sailor, see," he interrupted. "You know—girl in every port. I probably got kids all over the world."

I could imagine housewives all over Texas—and a few other states—dropping wet dishes or stitches in their knitting or whatever they were doing. My first impulse was to bang him over the head with the microphone, but that would mean trouble. I had once knocked out a foul-mouthed heckler during a sidewalk program, and so many chiseling lawyers crawled out of the woodwork that I promised myself I would let nothing bother me again. I walked away from the sailor, and switched to another subject for the rest of the show.

Then there was an opera singer who flew in from Chicago to sing with the Exposition orchestra, and who at the last minute refused to perform unless we supplied her with a raw egg. Now, eggs are often laid on even the best shows, but they are not kept handy around a studio. It seems the great soprano needed the egg to relax her throat muscles, and we barely got one to her in time. She gulped it down and came up with a high C.

The Exposition people might not have bothered to import celebrities had it not been for the fact that in Fort Worth, the rival city thirty-two miles away, Billy Rose was being paid a hundred thousand dollars to stage colossals that would pull the tourists away from us. Billy coined a devastating slogan, "Dallas for Education, Fort Worth for Entertainment," and he claimed he drew a million customers that year. Perhaps he did. We may have made a lot of mistakes in choosing names and faces for our entertainment, but Billy Rose missed a bet he still has nightmares about.

He was auditioning acts in Fort Worth one day, and heard a pretty girl sing a sad little torch song called "Gloomy Sunday."

"Miss," he said bluntly, "my advice to you is to forget it. Go home, get married and tend to your dishes and diapers."

Later Billy was dining in the Stork Club in New York—the Dallas and Fort Worth fairs had long since been forgotten—when the "Gloomy Sunday" girl came up to his table and gave him a kiss. She reminded him, in case he couldn't remember, that her name was Mary Martin.

It was also in Dallas that I proved to myself—I had harbored some doubts about it since my gasoline cocktail episode in high school—that my metabolism is not and never will be adjusted to the absorption of alcoholic liquors. One of the Midway restaurants gave an open house champagne party for the Exposition staff. The champagne was free—Clyde Vandeburg teasingly says I wouldn't have been there otherwise—and after the second glass I began giggling. The world was warm and intimate and wonderfully cockeyed, and I loved everybody, and the giggles turned to hysterical laughter. I simply could not control these shrieking spasms and by the time I was guided out of the place, to the embarrassment of all concerned, I was sobbing like a barroom drunk who's just heard about Eliza crossing the ice. I look at champagne now as though it were the H-bomb, and I rarely try anything else that has alcohol in it.

ii

The Dallas Exposition was still making the cash registers rattle during the late summer of 1936 when Clyde Vandeburg, no longer the unruffled cowhand with loping walk and steady nerves, began showing unmistakable signs that it was time to take the herd over the hills to bigger pastures. The job in Dallas was done.

In San Francisco, almost two thousand miles west, the city's business leaders were organizing a world's fair—with an opening planned for the spring of 1939—and they wanted an expert for the build-up. Van got the job against some formidable competition and went to California to get started. I stayed on in Dallas, knowing I still had much to learn, but one day there came this telegram:

> San Francisco World Fair needs radio director. If you are still as crazy as I think you are, you will take the job. As ever,
>
> Vandeburg

"As ever." I knew what he meant. As new and exciting and challenging as ever. Analyzing my unrestrained work with people at the microphone once, Van said I was operating "in a meringue world." It was just that. Fragile, sweet, hollow, whipped with air and nothing more solid than the white of an egg. But where else could a young man on a cracker budget get meringue every day? Van knew I would come running, with no reservations at all. I was betting on him. Lois again asked me about the salary, of course, and once more I had to tell her I didn't care.

"Does it really matter what I get?" I asked.

"Of course not," she said. And she meant it.

We arrived in San Francisco in 1937, and I was soon involved in the usual larceny—trying to steal free air time to promote an enterprise that was unabashedly commercial. The problem in San Francisco was unique in many ways. At that point—with the actual fair-opening more than two years away—big dredges were busy out in the middle of San Francisco Bay, scooping up black sand to make an island. This artificial site would eventually be called Treasure Island, and would be connected to existing Yerba Buena Island with a causeway. The great span of the San Francisco Bay Bridge, which had been finished not too long before, would feed the traffic to the fair from Oakland and San Francisco.

It was a Herculean engineering undertaking to suck up millions of tons of sand and mud and rock and dump it on a shoal to make an island. The dredges clawed at the bottom every day, and the little nipple protruding from the water became a mound, then a flat plain. The causeway reached toward Yerba Buena and the artery soon began to pulse with trucks and cars and whirling mobile drums of wet cement.

But that's all there was for months.

Unlike San Diego, where beautiful buildings already graced Balboa Park, or Dallas, where the stage had already been set when we got there, there was nothing to talk about at San Francisco. We had blueprints and pictures and mock-ups and not much else. Consequently we resorted to some completely spurious devices to get network plugs now and then.

Among other things, we ordered an enormous cake and sent it to the late Major Bowes in New York with the nefarious idea that he might mention us on his famed Amateur Hour. Two weeks later Bowes sent me this telegram: "Cake damaged. Arrived in 2000 pieces. What shall I do?"

"Invite 2000 people to your show and let 'em eat cake," I wired back.

Perhaps it wasn't a clever answer at all. Major Bowes didn't invite anyone for cake and the Exposition finance department, which was then struggling along on a spaghetti-thin budget, found the cake item as indigestible as it had been for Major Bowes.

The year 1937 was a year to remember.

General Franco crushed the opposition and became dictator of Spain. The Japanese shelled and sank the United States gunboat "Panay," the first shadow of dreadful things to come.

Adolf Hitler washed out the Versailles Treaty, and Amelia Earhart, the world's foremost aviatrix, vanished forever in the South Seas. And Miss Sally Rand, whose parabolic fans were more or less synonymous with the world's fair, came to San Francisco, a cheerful omen, like the first robin or the umpire's "play ball."

Miss Rand, who had an uncanny appreciation of the value of newspaper column inches, happily agreed to go along with whatever nonsense we could concoct to spread the name of the Golden Gate International Exposition. With an inspired suggestion from Carl Wallen, then chief photographer for the fair, Sally said she would create a new dance. She would shield her milk-white body with living peacock feathers and would call it the Peacock Waltz. Once done, I would get Miss Rand to my microphone, describe each and every little movement and thus break the news to the world.

Unfortunately, there were no live peacocks to be had. The plumed beauties were out of season in the city's Golden Gate Park, and the outraged directors of the San Francisco Zoo would have none of their dignified birds dragged into the nomenclature of ecdysia. And anyway, they added, peacocks never spread their feathers unless they are annoyed or excited.

"She'll excite 'em all right," Wallen said.

The promise was not enough, and Sally eventually wound up on Treasure Island with a stuffed peacock that had glass eyes and stuffings leaking out of a torn taxidermist's seam. She went to work for us as the wind and dust blew across the bleak sand spit of an island, stripping a bit here and there, and leading us to the moment of truth. But there was no music or sound except an occasional squawk from a seagull and the grunts of surprise as three workmen stared and fell off a scaffold. The stiff breeze caught the peacock by the feathers and opened another stitch or two. Sally's hair stood out like a windsock, and with a word that ladies rarely use she plucked up her undies and reorganized herself back to her hotel.

There was no radio interview about this abortive milestone in the art of the strip-tease, and not a line in the news, and Sally went elsewhere with her rippling skin.

Much later I picked up a copy of *Look* magazine and in it was an enticing spread about Miss Sally Rand and her symmetry. One caption read: "The bare blonde dancer has a new dance and it isn't the minuet." There was a photo of Sally rehearsing her new routine, and she was holding something soft and fragile in her fingers, something that would apply just the provocative but proper degree of censorship. It was a peacock feather fan—and she called her new act "The Peacock Dance." There was not one word, alas, about the San Francisco world's fair.

iii

The eternal triangle is not necessarily a man and wife with a lover on the side.

In my case, the triangle began developing with the news that Lois was pregnant—ah, those rainy winter nights in San Francisco—and that the baby would be born sometime in November. Every couple reacts differently to the wonder of reproduction, and the seeming miracle that gives them a son or daughter of their own flesh. Lois and I knew that we wanted children, for whatever reason. We knew that a child would bring responsibilities to which neither of us had given much thought. I was making three hundred dollars a month, and we were in no position to afford such luxuries as baby sitters, a larger apartment, a second car, or perhaps a nurse.

But these or other drawbacks seemed unimportant, and we happily checked off the months.

It was reasonable and natural for me to want a son—as most fathers do—and my memory echoed a Christopher Morley verse I had liked in college:

> *There is no prince or prelate*
> *I envy—no, not one;*
> *No evil can befall me—*
> *By God, I have a son!*

On November 20, just a week before our second wedding anniversary, Lois went to Children's Hospital on California Street and gave birth to a son. The boy was delivered by a fine obstetrician named Dr. Henry Stephenson, and I can credit him with encouraging us to have other children right away. He didn't put it just that way, of course, but he did say: "Art, my bill for this baby will be $150, but you will get a discount with each succeeding one." I am unable to resist a bargain, and I quickly figured that if I bestirred myself I would eventually be getting babies for nothing. There might even be a refund. It was an interesting idea, as you can see.

We named our boy Arthur Jack Linkletter.

It is every man's privilege to indulge his vanity and perpetuate his name by calling a boy junior. We thought it over for a while, and both of us felt that to name him Art Linkletter, Jr. might impose a handicap, to say nothing of setting up psychological barriers that might plague him for the rest of his life. We ended up in a compromise and called the boy Arthur Jack Linkletter. He was Jack from the time he could crawl —and he is still Jack today.

In recent years, because of my work with children on the House Party show, I have written two books—*Kids Say the Darndest Things* and *The Secret World of Kids*—and in these volumes I naturally mentioned my own children many times. But in this autobiography—and I am sure that Jack and the others, Dawn, Robert, Sharon and Diane, will be relieved to hear it—there will be only occasional references to them. They may want to write their own autobiographies some day, and I would not want to be accused of having stolen all the material.

I remember one incident about Jack, though, and I mention it here only because it reminds me of the San Francisco world's fair days.

In Hollywood, when we finally got out of the red and the future looked reasonably secure, Lois and I bought a large house and employed a maid to help us with the children. At mealtimes, when we wanted to call the maid, we had a funny ritual in which Lois would press a buzzer while I simultaneously pushed my finger against the nose of the youngest child. The buzzer would sound, of course, and all of us would exclaim about the magic electricity in the baby's nose. We played this silly little game with each new baby, until all five of them had outgrown it, and there came a sad day when I knew there would be no more tiny noses to press.

Before that, though, Jack asked one evening: "Dad, did you press my nose, too, when I was a baby?"

"No, son," I said. "When you were little in San Francisco I had neither buzzer nor maid. And when you wanted something I got up and got it for you myself."

We not only had no buzzers or maids, we were lucky to have a car so I could get to work, and only by squeezing did we manage to put a few dollars in the bank for emergencies.

It bothered me to be earning only three hundred dollars a month when I felt that my experience entitled me to more, but it simply wasn't available in the fair budget at the time. In any case it was not hard to rationalize that I was not only getting a free post-graduate course in my business, but I was having fun doing it.

I would be distorting the facts if I said there were not disappointments and headaches and flops in the two-year period that preceded the opening of the fair. There were times when I had to lock up my tongue to keep it from saying things I would most certainly regret, and that might have put me out on the sidewalk before I was ready to go. There were also times when some of our elaborate promotion ideas backfired with tragic results.

I remember sitting in Clyde Vandeburg's office with Richard Halliburton, the handsome and romantic young man whose unique travel books were best sellers. Opening-day ceremonies were always a problem, and in the search for offbeat attractions more than one fair expert has reached the nervous breakdown stage.

We thought we had a winner in Halliburton. The plan was to have him go to China, buy a large and colorful junk and sail it across the Pacific. He was certain that he could arrive outside the Golden Gate on opening day and his triumphant entry—up to that time no man had ever attempted such a risky feat—would officially launch the fair. We would meet him offshore and get an exclusive report on the trip for a network show. Halliburton was a nationally known name and his presence at Treasure Island was bound to attract thousands of people to whom he was the symbol of daring adventure.

"You have no doubts about the trip?" Vandeburg asked.

"None at all," Halliburton said.

I can still see him sitting there—lean, bronzed by the sun, impeccably groomed and tailored. The starched cuffs of his shirt protruded two inches from the sleeves, and there was a silk handkerchief tucked into one cuff. Here was a modern d'Artagnan, and we had him. We shook hands and wished him good sailing, and he walked jauntily out the door. He went to China, outfitted the junk, and steered it out into the sea toward California. Neither he nor his boat were ever seen again.

iv

As time passed, old friends began filtering into San Francisco to case the big show and perhaps get in on the ground floor. Sally Rand, her ruffled fans smoothed by the new exotic beauty of Treasure Island, signed a contract for a midway attraction where semi-nude cowgirls would frolic around a new kind of ranch. Billy Rose came out from New York to plan an Aquacade. Betty Grable, Bob Hope and Eddie Cantor came to town to help us with the build-up. The late Tom Breneman, whose breakfast club program was then one of the top national shows, often contributed his ad-lib genius to the cause.

I was under the impression that my radio department, during those long months of preparation, had done more than its share to spread the name of San Francisco around the world. We were getting more than ten thousand dollars' worth of free air time every week on local and national shows, and could count more than six thousand broadcasts in which the fair had been mentioned, or discussed in detail. I had handled most of these programs myself and I was working sixteen hours a day. One day I was summoned to the office of Harris Connick, then general manager of the fair. As I recall, I had just de-scribed the coming exposition from an airplane on a coast to coast network. I thought this had been quite a feat, considering that it was a very foggy day, and I couldn't see a thing except the back of the pilot's head. Perhaps Mr. Connick was going to give me a raise.

"Mr. Linkletter," he said coldly, "I regret to say that in my opinion your work has been dull, without imagination and more or less useless. And your suggestions for an opening-day broadcast are stupid."

The raise went out the window right then, and I was stunned. A sarcastic crack was bouncing around on the tip of my tongue, but I hung on to it. "Mr. Connick," I said, turning the other cheek, "what do *you* suggest for opening day?"

"Well," he said, "you're familiar with the Golden Gate Bridge. You know that each suspension cable has a different tension, and when the wind blows in from the ocean these cables make a musical tone."

It was true that the cables did make a sound when the wind hit them. I had heard it myself. "Yes, sir," I said.

"Now, my idea is this," he went on. "You pick out the cables that have the eight notes of the scale, put a microphone on each one, and run the wires into a control board with keys. Presto—you have the world's largest harp, and you could maybe get Artur Rubinstein to play 'California, Here I Come.' Magnificent, eh?"

I looked him right in the eye, and said: "Mr. Connick, you're nuts!"

He looked me right in the eye and said: "Mr. Linkletter, you're fired!"

It seemed like a catastrophe then, for I had saved very little out of my salary. But this jolting and painful turn of events forced me to change my personal timetable and soon I was earn-

ing considerably more—I told myself with grim satisfaction—
than Mr. Connick. Many times since I have blessed him for
firing me, but in the back of my mind there persists a nagging
little thought. Do you suppose someone *could* wire up those
cables on the bridge and play "California, Here I Come"?

9. Storm Out of San Simeon

THERE ARE INTROSPECTIVE evenings now and then, when I sit alone in my den at home, and wonder whether I have achieved the goals I set for myself twenty years ago.

Perhaps I have.

It is reassuring to know that half the call girls from Los Angeles to Chicago have made my name and program, along with my announcer Jack Slattery, a symbol of security against the predatory tactics of the gendarmes in the big hotels, or house dicks as they are called in the lingo of the traveling salesman.

There are savants who will argue that this is true immortality, but I must say it isn't what I had in mind when I was fired from the San Francisco fair.

Jerry Bundsen of the San Francisco *Chronicle* told me recently that he met me on Market Street in San Francisco one afternoon, shortly after my unhappy showdown with Harris Connick. He says I was not the slightest bit despondent about this calamity—which is true—and that I said gaily: "Best thing that ever happened to me. I'm going to make a million dollars in the next five years. Starting right now."

I don't remember making this rash forecast, but one point was clear in my mind. I knew I would never again be on a payroll, working for a single employer on a regular job. I also knew that thereafter I would be working, not for glory, but for money. I had long since passed the apprentice stage. I had handled thousands of broadcasts, I knew my business, and someone was going to pay for my know-how.

One of my first projects as a free-lancer was a spectacular pageant called Cavalcade of the Golden West. This production was a history of the Far West in twenty-five scenes, with three hundred players. The late Samuel G. Blythe, the famed author and *Saturday Evening Post* editor, collaborated with me on the script, and when he broke his leg—we were about half finished at the time—I took the work to his home in Monterey, 130 miles south of San Francisco. He was a gallant and wise man, and when I saw him for the last time he gave me a large photograph of himself on which he had written: "To a young man who's going places—from an old man who's been there."

There is some irony in the fact that my first major project as an independent was a creative writing undertaking that had nothing to do with radio.

Professor Florence Smith of San Diego State notwithstanding, the Cavalcade show was not only an artistic success—or so the critics said—but it had the cash registers ringing like a burglar alarm. Seven thousand people went to the opening, and when the news got around, the show touched a twelve thousand dollar weekly gross in the first two weeks. Not even the crustiest historians would have bet that Custer's Last Stand —and we staged the scene to the last man and bullet—would outdraw the nude maidens lassoing the yokels at Sally Rand's midway ranch attraction. But Custer did it. We gradually pulled away from the bare lassies—it seems there were thousands of people who hadn't seen a horse for years—and eventually hit a fifty thousand dollar weekly gross.

There was only one little cloud of dust on this bright blue Cavalcade horizon. The Exposition management had agreed to pay me two thousand for my contribution to the script. Weeks went by, and the money was rolling into the box office, but I couldn't collect. I was in an uncomfortable position—doing business every day with the executives—but I was also irked because they kept stalling me.

One day I got attachment papers and headed for the Cavalcade office, accompanied by a deputy sheriff.

I was prepared to put a lien on the horses in the show, or anything else that was movable. But the news of my intent preceded me, and when I got there they had a certified check waiting. It was not idle chatter when my friend, the late A. L.

(Red) Vollman, who produced the Cavalcade, said: "When Link chases down money that's coming to him, he makes Buffalo Bill look like a monkey riding a mule."

Anyone examining my frenzied schedule during that period would conclude, from a surface reading, at least, that I had solved the secret of perpetual motion. I was pursuing a little bit of everything, like a dog at a cat show. I was averaging eighteen shows a week, and *Variety*, the show business paper, called me a "One Man Dynamo" who, according to their spies, was averaging seven hundred dollars a week.

I was no longer a mere hired hand.

I was Art Linkletter—Master of Ceremonies.

In one definition, at least, Webster defines a master of ceremonies as "an official at solemn services charged with the duty of seeing that all the rites are correctly executed," but I have since made a couple of changes in that definition. There was never anything solemn about my early shows—if anything, they were more on the riotous side—and my rights were certainly executed, a fate that actually should have befallen some of the characters I met.

One of my first such shows, broadcast in front of the Federal Building on Treasure Island, was called "What Do You Think?" The format was simple. I chose a current events subject—usually highly controversial—and then asked for opinions from anyone willing to talk. I quickly learned three disturbing things about people when there are controversies involved. First, the average man is astonishingly intolerant when he is arguing a pet belief. Second, he listens to the opposing view only because he's just waiting to whack you with his own opinion. And third—and this has always baffled me— no matter what was said by either side I would be personally blamed by my listening audience. I was in the same position as the umpire at the ball game. Always the villain.

My first mishap in this field came when I stopped people and asked them whether they were going to vote for President Franklin D. Roosevelt or his opponent, Wendell Willkie. I kept count of the votes, and at the end of a two-week period announced on the air that Willkie was far out in front. The shock wave that rolled out of the fair's executive offices nearly carried me out into the ocean, and I was ordered—and I mean ordered—not to mention Mr. Willkie or any other politicians again.

My immediate reaction was to advise the brass that this was a free country, and that no stuffy vice presidents could put handcuffs on me. But I didn't, and that was just as well. I had no idea how many Democrats were hiding behind rocks and trees and not telling me that Willkie couldn't make it. I was certainly not as sagacious as a thirteen-year-old boy on the House Party show when I asked him to define the word "politician."

"Oh, that's a person who solves problems that wouldn't be there," he said, "if there weren't any politicians."

I suppose I was naïve in some ways.

I had no idea that these public opinion programs attracted Commies, Fascists, wobblies, chronic troublemakers and other crackpots, until one newspaper columnist said as much. "There is a radio program," he wrote, mentioning my name, "that has innocently become a vehicle for Communist and Nazi propaganda and the public is getting a distorted impression."

I was angry and hurt, of course. I believed in the principle of free thought and free speech, and I felt that it was a healthy thing to have people of all races and faiths say exactly what they thought. And so I stubbornly fought for the show, and went on with it. I had no idea of the dangers involved, or that a day was coming when I wished I had never asked that simple question: "What do you think?"

ii

On December 1, 1939, I became the father of a baby girl. We named her Dawn, not only because she was born in Children's Hospital at daybreak, but because she had the soft and lovely color of the morning that heralds the rising sun. I am incurably sentimental, as you can see, about little girls.

We broke the news to our friends with a cartoon quiz we designed ourselves—one drawing showed the sun rising over the crest of a hill—and asked them to guess the baby's name by looking at the picture. Even our slow-witted acquaintances —and there are some—had no trouble with this puzzle, and some retaliated by suggesting that, as a new father, I was now qualified to work the Dawn Patrol. I did, too. In between shows I occasionally paced the floor with this tiny bundle of pink froth, and I'm glad I did. In fact, having just received the cheerful news that Dawn has become the mother of twins—she is now Mrs. John Andrew Zweyer—I have volunteered my services as an old pro and am ready to go back on the Dawn Patrol as I did many years ago.

The birth of our daughter had a surprising effect on Mother Linkletter, and she wrote a note saying she was coming to visit us in San Francisco.

Knowing how sedentary she was, shying away from people and the outside world, I was a little nonplused. We had invited her to come on other occasions, but she always pleaded that she had to stay home and take care of Father Linkletter. He was in his seventies now and was beginning to feel the inexorable fatigue of old age, even though he was still running the little shoe shop on the ground floor of the apartment building in which they lived.

I wanted Mother Linkletter to know she was welcome and, rather than sending a note, I picked up the phone and called our intermediary in Grabell's Grocery next door. My parents still refused to have a phone, though I offered to pay for it, and when we wanted to deliver messages we sent them via kindly Mr. Grabell.

Mother got our invitation, but she didn't tell us her plans. Consequently she arrived at our apartment—clutching the shiny new suitcase we had given her—when I was out of town doing a broadcast from the northern California city of Chico. She and Lois chatted about family affairs for a day or so, but then ran out of conversation. The second evening, as Mother was reading the Bible, Lois got out a pack of cards and began playing solitaire.

She suddenly became aware that Mother had closed the Bible, and was staring at her in righteous indignation. Lois squirmed under this silent condemnation, put the cards away and slunk into her bedroom. Mother had been given a bed in the same room because our two children had the only other bedroom, but that evening she primly curled up on a couch in the living room. She simply would not sleep in the same room with a sinful woman who played cards, and the following day, still upset, Mother packed up and went home.

My mother and Lois eventually made peace, and became good friends.

I tried—then and later—to rationalize her behavior, but I'm afraid I never quite succeeded. I knew that both she and Father Linkletter had always had an almost frightening obsession about such simple pleasures as cards, theaters, dancing and liquor. They had also inflicted these fanaticisms on me, and up to the time I was graduated from high school they had never knowingly permitted me inside a movie theater. I had to sneak into a movie—as I did the time I won the Kiwanis Club prize—and

I never told them how much I loved to dance. They were so bigoted about these things—and I tried to excuse them on the grounds of ignorance—that they shut out all reason. Thus they also shut out everyone who did not conform, and they closed the door on life itself. It is no wonder that they almost lost the only son they ever had.

iii

In the spring of 1940, as a sort of celebration for the arrival of Dawn Linkletter, I wrote the script for a new pageant called "Cavalcade of America." This was produced at the San Francisco world's fair when the big show went into a second year and, I admit modestly, was as financially rewarding—both to me and the fair's administration—as the "Cavalcade of the West."

But even this seemingly innocuous subject got me embroiled in an unpleasant feud which proved that you can't monkey around with history as long as there are bristling defenders who won't let you get away with it. I had a scene in which George Washington gives his memorable Farewell Address, and uses the word "Republic." I took the liberty of changing the word to "Democracy," thinking it was more in keeping with the times, but I had not counted on the vigilant ladies of the Daughters of the American Revolution.

Washington's winter at Valley Forge was a Florida sun tan compared to the freeze I got from the DAR. They had a special session at their regular council meeting and one of their belligerent spokesmen, a Mrs. Joseph Taylor Young, implied that as a historian I was in the low, low IQ department.

"A Democracy," she said, "means a direct rule by the people, "but that is not what we have in America. It is an ideal to talk

about and strive for but today, as in Washington's time, we
are a Republic. If Washington's speech has to be cut, let it be
cut legitimately, not paraphrased."

Once again I retreated. I am cowardly indeed when it comes
to ladies on the warpath, especially if I might be wrong. I
phoned Sam Blythe in Monterey—he had collaborated on this
script, too—and we agreed to a compromise surrender. We
eliminated both words, Republic and Democracy, and substi-
tuted "representative government by the people." As Rod
Serling says, it's all a matter of semantics, and I am the last man
in the world to be anti-semantic.

The "Cavalcade of America" had one other important consequence with a much happier ending.

To a front row seat one day came Mr. Mervyn LeRoy of
Hollywood and Metro-Goldwyn-Mayer. In those days, if your
ambitions were aimed at that land of big pay—as mine were—
LeRoy was one of the men with a check-writing machine that
could knock out six figures without stripping a gear.

When the performance ended that afternoon, one of the
staff came to my office and said that LeRoy was in the lobby
and wanted to see me. To me this was comparable to a summons
from the White House, and I stopped admiring my new
secretary's hair-do long enough to run down the stairs. LeRoy
was a round-faced, stocky young man with dark hair and eyes
that were snapping at me like slingshots.

"Art," he said, "I've just seen your show and it's great.
Hollywood needs creative talent and I think you've got it.
Could you come down to the studio and bring me some other
samples of your work?"

Could I? I would have crawled the whole distance over
broken glass. I scrambled around and packed up copies of
everything I had written, and flew to Hollywood. I rented a
car and drove miles to the MGM lot at Culver City, and

presently I was being ushered into LeRoy's private office. The room was not much larger than the rotunda at the San Francisco City Hall, and at the far end, within easy walking distance, the great man sat at his desk. It was not exactly a desk. It was a jewelry counter at Cartier's—a long fortification of polished mahogany and glass with not a scrap of paper in sight.

I gingerly laid my fourteen pounds of literature on the glistening surface of the desk. The package included everything I had ever done, including grammar school essays, and I could see him blinking a little.

"How much money are you making now, Art?" he asked.

I did some lightning calculation and then doubled the amount. "Oh . . . maybe forty thousand or so," I said.

"Forty thousand?" he said. "A mere beginning. You ought to make a hundred thousand here at the end of the first year. More after that, naturally."

I was reeling, and he knew it.

"Tell you what, Art," he said, "I'll run over this material tonight. I'll call you at your hotel in the morning and then we'll have another talk."

I floated back to my room at the Knickerbocker Hotel in Hollywood, and I waited. I waited all day and at five o'clock, to stop my twitching and floor-pacing, I called his office. "So sorry," a secretary said. "Mr. LeRoy has gone to New Orleans." I waited another twenty-four hours and phoned again. "Oh, Mr. Linkletter," the voice said, "these are very trying days for Mr. LeRoy. He had to go to Hong Kong." I checked out of the hotel and went back to San Francisco. I tied myself down for two days, then phoned again. Mr. LeRoy was incommunicado in London, but he had not forgotten me.

Well . . . I could wait it out. I could always grow a new set of fingernails. After all, a hundred thousand a year. Maybe more. My name on the movie screen. Lunch every day at the Derby. Conferences with Joan Fontaine, Ginger Rogers, Vivien Leigh, Joan Crawford. An Oscar.

Ten years later I went to a Hollywood party and there he was, greeting me as though I were Louis B. Mayer himself.

"You know, Art," he said, "I've been thinking about how Hollywood needs creative writing and—"

"Yes, I know," I said. "If I come to MGM I ought to make at least a hundred thousand a year."

"Amazing!" he said. "You must be on my wave-length."

"Oh, it's nothing," I said. "But please don't hold the job open. I'm making two hundred thousand now, and I don't really need it."

Merv and I have since become good friends, have worked together on a number of public service projects, and have laughed about this affair many times. Matter of fact, I now know how these things happen. I have interviewed talented people myself, and I have had every good intention of doing something about it. But if there are delays—a trip out of town, a business meeting—enthusiasm wears off or something new comes along. If I had had an agent—I didn't have one then or for the next twenty years—he would have lived in a sleeping bag outside LeRoy's office until a decision was made. And I might have gone to work at MGM just long enough to get lost in its labyrinthine vaults.

iv

Meanwhile, back in the salt mines at San Francisco, I kept up the frantic digging for money and fame.

I was emceeing a nighttime show called "Who's Dancing Tonight?" at the big downtown hotels, and at the St. Francis one evening, I met a beautiful and gracious star named Ina Claire. She had just retired from the stage to marry William Ross Wallace, Jr., a San Francisco businessman, and we had a saucy interview about show business.

After we went off the air, she took me aside and said: "Art, you're a natural comedian, but never try to be a joke-teller or a comic. Stay as you are with the light touch, and some day you'll be a star."

Ina's praise strengthened my uncertain ego, and I never forgot what she did for me that night. Subsequently, on this same "Who's Dancing Tonight?" show, I got similar encouragement from Georgie Jessel and Eddie Cantor, and they were so positive about my future that I almost began to believe it myself. When the time came to make the break from San Francisco, it was the commendation from these three great entertainers that gave me the courage and the optimism to try the major league.

Along with "Who's Dancing Tonight?" I was also doing "Treasure Time," a variety show from the fair grounds; a radio cookbook quiz for a sausage manufacturer; a half-hour interview for the Roma Wine Company, also at the fair, and a sidewalk-reporter program for a shoe store.

The latter show was broadcast from a street corner on Market Street, San Francisco's main thoroughfare, and, frankly, it was not the spirited sort of offering that would make a national sponsor reach for his checkbook. One day, gabbing with a pedestrian who was almost as bored as I was, I heard a siren in the distance.

"Listen, folks!" I cried. "We interrupt our show for a *real* life-and-death drama. Here comes an ambulance . . . siren screaming . . . tearing down Market Street at sixty miles an hour. Some poor human has been hurt . . . and there he goes to the Emergency Hospital! Boy, that ambulance really burns up the pavement. But wait—right behind is another car . . .

and it's gaining. It's catching up . . . it's full of lawyers . . . I can hear them yelling: 'Sue! Sue! Sue!' "

I was young and cocky enough to think this was a pretty funny ad lib, but the San Francisco Bar Association dropped the roof on me the next day and deluged my sponsors with threats about getting rid of Linkletter—or else. Lamely I tried to explain they were undoubtedly lawyers from Oakland—San Francisco's rival city across the bay—but my sponsor didn't think that was cute, either. Turned out he lived in Oakland. I was on probation for weeks afterward, and I never again made cracks about ambulance chasers.

It was on the same Market Street corner, at the intersection of Mason Street, that a disastrous ad lib very nearly ruined the budding radio career of a young man named Jack Webb. As Jack tells it, he was standing on the sidewalk interviewing people who were wildly celebrating V-J Day, and he had the tough luck to grab a sailor just off a returning battleship.

"Hi, sailor," he said, "this is the American Broadcasting Company on a coast to coast network. Would you mind telling me what you're going to do now that the war's over?"

"Why, sure, pal," the sailor said. "I'm gonna find me a girl and take her to bed."

Jack says: "The sailor left me standing there with my bridge-work melted and a sizable hunk of dead air." But he recovered, and went from there to Hollywood to make four or five million dollars with "Dragnet."

Perhaps that Market Street block had a jinx on it. Because it was also there, in the Telenews Theater, that I was hit by a couple of blockbusters that ended my love affair with controversial subjects. The show was the same one I originated on Treasure Island, "What Do You Think?", and my sponsor was the Albert S. Samuels Company, a jewelry firm known as "The House of Lucky Wedding Rings."

The show started harmlessly enough. The format was identical to the one I used at the fair—an important current events question on which people could give their opinion, pro or con. I purposely refrained from making advance announcement of the subject matter because I did not want the house packed with hand-picked orators representing pressure groups. We were going along fine the first month or two, and for a strictly local show were getting some remarkable ratings.

Then came that horrible evening when the question was: "What do you think of Adolf Hitler?"

The war was on in Europe, the Nazi armies had begun their terrible march of death and destruction, and it was only a question of time when the United States would be involved in the conflict. Everybody was talking about Hitler, and he was a natural subject for an open forum.

The first volunteer speaker that night was a big, tough truck driver who got up, dusted off his hands as though he had just kayoed a rival in a street brawl and said: "Hitler is nuts. He's a jerk who's got a lot of other jerks hypnotized, and we oughta hire some hood to rub him out before he gets us mixed up in his crummy war." He sat down, and another volunteer stood up. He was a meek, pale little man who looked as though he'd crawled out of a damp basement, and his voice was small and soft. "Mr. Linkletter," he said, "I have given this question considerable thought. My carefully considered opinion is that Adolf Hitler is the greatest man who ever lived, not excepting Jesus Christ."

He started to sit down, but he never made it. The truck driver grabbed his necktie and gave it a violent jerk. Two rows away, another man made a crack and was rewarded with a short left to the chin by a stranger alongside him. People began shouting and shoving and climbing over the seats. It was a shambles, and we needed help from the police to calm things down.

The real victim, though, was Art Linkletter.

One weekly newspaper called me a Communist. Another said I was a Fascist. One civic organization demanded that I be investigated by the FBI. A second group pressured the sponsor to dump me.

The wreckage had just been cleared away when I unfortunately chose to discuss newspapers and their impact on people. Midway during the show, a man in the audience took on the late William Randolph Hearst, and when he finished a somewhat scathing speech, I looked over the audience and said: "Now, is there anyone who would like to speak up for Mr. Hearst?"

There was an ominous silence and I repeated the question. No one stood up.

"Well . . ." I said, "I'll be happy to continue the discussion on my next program, and I invite Hearst supporters to come and speak up."

The news about this broadcast got to the Hearst castle at San Simeon almost before I was out of the theater, and as of that moment, as far as the Hearst newspapers were concerned, Art Linkletter ceased to exist. My name was not mentioned in these journals for more than two years, and none of my programs were listed in the radio logs. That hurt. One Hearst publisher who was and still is a close friend, told me in confidence that Hearst felt I had purposely planned the broadcast as an attack on him, and that I had "packed" the audience with anti-Hearst people. This was not true, of course, but I thought afterward how ironic it was that this was the only show of that whole series in which there were not articulate and noisy speakers for both sides. I don't blame Hearst for being angry about that, and I was afraid he would never relent and lift the ban.

The Telenews show eventually became too inflammable for both me and the sponsor, and it was abandoned by mutual consent.

The punishment from San Simeon would have been enough to knock out even the best local show—especially in a city with two powerful Hearst newspapers. I almost admitted to myself that I was hanging on the ropes, and I was sitting up half the night sketching out new show ideas that would keep me going in San Francisco.

It was then that Hollywood called.

I was afraid of the town. It was the Big Time, but it was also the graveyard of dead dreams. But I could still hear Ina Claire's cheery words and I remembered that Georgie Jessel had said: "Look, kid, you'll make it big. I know what I'm talking about." If I wasn't ready now, I would never be. Lois and I packed our bags, and shipped our furniture south. We put the babies in the car, and we started the long drive down the coast road. Had our tomorrow dawned at last?

10. Nine, Ten—and Out!

> *Kids are not alone in saying the darndest things.
> I was interviewing a newly-married young
> woman on the House Party show one morning,
> and I inquired how she had met her husband.*
>
> *"At a costume party," she said. "I was dressed
> as a Spanish senorita."*
>
> *"And how was he dressed?" I asked.*
>
> *"Why . . . he wasn't dressed at all," she said
> innocently.*

OUR INTRODUCTION to the dizzy and fascinating world of
Hollywood, quite naturally enough, was at a party. It was not
a costume party, as it happens, although a number of cele-
brated guests were wearing their usual masks.

The old-time parties in Hollywood, Beverly Hills and Bel-
Air were institutions—if you were ready for an institution—and
a forty thousand dollar tab merely represented a few weeks'
work for the big stars in that low tax period. People coaxed
and schemed to get invitations for these lavish affairs—they
were as coveted as a World Series box—and more than one
million-dollar deal was conceived alongside a marble pool, or in
an upstairs boudoir.

But by the time we moved to the movie capital, most of the
big spenders had either withdrawn from the arena, or were

looking for fresh plasma for their anemic bank accounts. There was still one titan of the cocktail-canapé mob who entertained as though he were living on borrowed time. As a matter of fact, he was.

His name was A. Atwater Kent, a little sparrow of a man who had made millions in the radio and electronics industry, and who had come to California to retire. He was about sixty-three years old then, soft-spoken, intensely lonely and shy, a man whose natty dress each day suggested a schoolboy going to graduation exercises.

Kent's parties were divided into groups.

Group One was for big business executives, most of them from downtown Los Angeles, and they got spaghetti and meat balls. Group Two was composed of average Hollywood celebrities, and the *pièce de résistance* was chicken. Group Three consisted of the elite corps—nationally known authors and editors, opera singers, famed artists and the high-bracket motion picture and television stars. They were fed *filet mignons* with mushrooms. In each classification there were usually so many guests that Kent, personally greeting each one at the door, merely nodded his head and smiled, like a little mechanical man. He was far too abstracted to listen to what anyone said, and so it became a game with some of the Hollywood wags to invent outrageous greetings as Kent welcomed them to the party.

As a typical example, one popular comedian once said: "Hello, Mr. Kent. Sorry I'm a little late, but my wife was run over by a steamroller today."

Kent replied: "How nice. Please come right in."

There were infinite variations on this gag, and apparently Kent never caught on. Anyway, one of our friends in Los Angeles was Margaret "Maggie" Ettinger, an exceedingly successful public relations operator whose aunt happens to be

Miss Louella Parsons. Maggie was often engaged by Kent to make up a guest list for his parties—she was always *au courant* about who was in and who was out—and once in a while she would thoughtfully slip in the name of a newly-arrived friend who was just breaking the ice in Hollywood. One day, not long after we moved from San Francisco, Maggie added our names to a Group Three list, and in due course, we got our invitations.

"We have arrived socially," I said jokingly to Lois.

"Yes," she said. "Along with five thousand others."

To digress for a moment, since this is a sort of Inside Linkletter, there are a few things my press agents haven't mentioned about me. One is that I am a light-turner-offer. We have seventeen rooms in our house, and it seems to me they are always lit up like a ballpark, especially when they are empty. I prowl around like a house detective and turn off the lights, and it gives me a warm, satisfied feeling to know that I am being thrifty.

This habit could be traced back to my boyhood when, more often than not, Father Linkletter couldn't pay the electricity bill, and I had to help hustle up the money. But it is much more likely that I can credit this electrical frugalness to A. Atwater Kent.

He didn't know me from Yehudi Menuhin the night we went to his party. But while the third army was sopping up his costly booze, I was strolling outside, and I found him wandering around alone among the trees of his vast estate. He was so uncommunicative for two or three minutes that I was sure he was mulling over some multi-million-dollar deal, and perhaps he wished that I would go back to the snack table and leave him alone.

"You want to know something interesting, young man?" he said suddenly. "I have proved that when you have six or seven acres like this you can put maybe a dozen light bulbs in the trees at the right spots and light up the whole place."

"I never thought of it just like that," I said.

"Those bulbs," he went on, "only cost me a few cents a night to burn, and they save me the expense of hiring two night watchmen. Interesting, eh?"

I walked back to the party, where thirty waiters were just beginning to serve filet mignon and champagne, and I had something to think about. *That's how you get to be a millionaire*, I said to myself, and I've been watching those light bulbs at home ever since. Not that it does me any good.

I was enjoying one of Kent's choice steaks when a young woman with a notebook tapped me on the arm.

"You're fifth, Mr. Linkletter," she said, glancing down at the open page and making a check mark.

"Fifth what?" I asked.

"Well," she said, "we always like to organize a little entertainment for Mr. Kent . . . you know, volunteers . . . and you're fifth on the program."

"Really? What am I supposed to do?"

"Any little act you want. Ten or twelve minutes."

She began to move away, and I said: "Wait a minute. Who's first?"

She looked at her notebook. "First is a duet with Ginny Simms and Dinah Shore."

"Who goes second?"

"Edgar Bergen and Charlie McCarthy."

She had me rocking by this time, and I shakily asked her about act number three. "Oh . . . let's see," she said. "Ah, yes. George Burns is going to do one of his routines, and after him comes Jack Benny. Then you."

Bergen, Burns and Benny. Then me. I couldn't have been more stunned. "Honey," I said to Lois, "they're loaded with

BB's and they're going to riddle me right out of town on the first shot."

I had no act. Not for ten minutes or five minutes. Not at all. I felt like the man in front of the firing squad, waiting to get mowed down. I wished I had never heard of A. Atwater Kent. I wandered through the babbling crowd, searching for a friendly face, and I spotted Kay Kyser, the popular professor from the "College of Musical Knowledge." I explained my plight and he said: "There's Louella Parsons over there. If you could do a bit with her you've got it made."

I appraised Louella doubtfully. I had been introduced to her no less than eight or ten times, and each time her eyes would cloud and she would say: "I'm sorry. I didn't quite catch the name."

But this was no time to hesitate. I walked across the lawn and introduced myself again. I frankly told her my awkward situation and I pleaded with her to help me out. To my immense relief she laughed and said she thought it would be fun. It was. When my turn came, I staged a little game that involved transferring an orange back and forth from chin to chin. The contestants were Louella, Kay Kyser, Walter Slezak and a pretty young girl I picked out of the crowd. Her name was Ruth Roman and she was then a complete unknown.

I acted as timekeeper, referee and announcer for these trifling shenanigans—it was simply a variation of an old parlor game—and it was certainly something new for a Kent soiree. It was hilarious, in fact, and when the dignified Miss Parsons struggled with the orange the shrieks of laughter were probably heard for miles. Louella was gallant about the raillery, and I was off to a spectacular start in a town I had invaded with such trembling.

Kent invited me to his home often after that, but when illness struck him down there were no more parties. He died of cancer, and his passing marked the end of an era in Hollywood. He was kind and generous and, though few people got through to his lonely heart, hundreds of others still think of him as a generous host who never quite learned to enjoy the parties himself. I hope that the guardian of the gate—wherever Kent may have gone—remembered his name and said: "How nice to see you. Please come in."

ii

Louella Parsons, I'm happy to say, never forgot my name again, and we have been good friends ever since. Indeed, without any overtures from me, she used her influence with Hearst on my behalf, and as a result my name was taken off the publisher's blacklist. That reprieve boosted my morale because I was preparing to launch my new Hollywood shows, and I needed all the publicity I could get.

I made my debut with a program sponsored by my old friends of the Roma Wine Company.

It was what we loosely call a variety show, originating on the huge stage of the Earl Carroll theater restaurant on Sunset Boulevard. I planned to wander around interviewing people in the audience, or bringing them to the stage, and there was certain to be a number of celebrities to give the show a little lustre. I was convinced we would quickly get a high rating—as similar programs had in San Francisco—and that rich sponsors would be standing in line for my services.

Unfortunately I had not counted on competition of a biological nature.

When the late Earl Carroll composed the lyrical phrase for his theaters: "Through these portals pass the most beautiful girls in the world," he was not indulging in literary license. Carroll's chorus girls were uniformly dazzling, long-stemmed and satin-skinned, and the mysterious areas on their beautiful bodies were hidden by cloth patches not much larger than a band-aid. They were sexy, they were desirable, they were images beckoning to every aging Tantalus in Hollywood.

The bald-headed customers, impatiently waiting for the main attraction—the Carroll girls they had paid to see—never stopped eating or drinking long enough to notice that I was on stage. If ever a man died to a chorus of clinking glasses and rattling knives and forks, I did. The show was a ghastly flop, and after four appearances I was canceled out. The theater restaurant has since been renamed the Moulin Rouge, but I never go past it without remembering the personal disaster I encountered there. The only compensating thought I have is that fourteen years later I stood on that same stage—in the spring of 1955—and received a coveted Emmy for having the best daytime show in television.

When the Roma program folded, I hustled around and found another sponsor.

This time it was the Shell Oil Company, and we had an idea that simply could not miss. The show was to be called "Shell Goes to a Party," and I signed a thirteen-week contract at a thousand dollars a week. If the show was a hit on the West Coast, as I knew it would be, the company planned to give it national promotion and move it to the CBS coast-to-coast network.

Millions of Americans go to parties every weekend, and hostesses vacuum their brain cells for original ideas. Few of them can afford to import movie stars and orchestras at thirty or forty thousand dollars a clip, as A. Atwater Kent did, but they do come up with novel themes their guests will enjoy. My program was built on the premise that everyone enjoys a good party, and that if we offered something unique each week we would have a ready-made audience. Our audition record, in fact, was put together with tapes we had made at a University of Southern California fraternity barn dance, and on the strength of that somewhat crude presentation the show was bought by the J. Walter Thompson Company for Shell.

The first program was broadcast from a restaurant on La Cienega Boulevard—I had obviously not learned that restaurants are often lethal weapons—and the party in this instance was a reunion of wealthy sportsmen who owned and flew their own planes. They began gathering in the bar at six o'clock, three hours before our air time, and many of them were soothing the fatigue of a long flight with doubles on the rocks. They were rapidly gaining altitude when I got there, and by the time I started strolling among them with my microphone they were in outer space.

That party was an incredible clambake, and I was thankful that I did not have to fly back to Tucson or Denver or some other distant point with one of these characters at the controls.

I had to do some desperate ad libbing to keep things going, carefully stepping over pilots who had crash-landed on the floor, and the evening would have been a four-alarm catastrophe without some unexpected help from three amateur pilots who knew that liquor was not a navigation aid—Edgar Bergen, and Charlie Correll and Freeman Gosden, who made up the famed Amos and Andy team. These high-priced gentlemen generously contributed a couple of skits and filled out one of the most padded half hours of my young career.

Fortunately there were no cries of anguish from the agency people. They probably didn't hear the falling bodies in the background, or perhaps they had once been pilots themselves and knew how easy it was to get lost in the fog.

I was not taking any chances at this stage, though, and for

the following week I had arranged something less raucous. It was to be a campfire and marshmallow party at the beach, with the current Miss America as a special guest. The plan was to have my assistants pick up the gorgeous doll and throw her into the sea—a clever twist considering that bathing beauties, with the possible exception of Miss Esther Williams, had rarely been known to get their suits wet.

When we arrived at the beach with our equipment, there was a gray overcast reaching far out over the sea, and a southeast wind was blowing driftwood, leaves, seaweed and sand at our broadcasting site. Neighborhood delinquents, drawn by the publicity on the show, swarmed on the beach like locusts and stole our marshmallows and props until we chased them off.

The wind carried my voice out toward Catalina Island, and it also picked up hot ashes from our campfire and dumped them on our shivering guests.

I had that sick, empty feeling in my stomach and I knew that nothing short of a smashing climax would save this show. So I juggled my timetable and gave the signal for my men. They grabbed Miss America and carried her, squirming and squealing, toward the water as I followed behind with my mike trailing a long cord. The moment we left the bright circle of light from the campfire, the night turned very black and I tripped over a log. The Columbia Broadcasting System suddenly disappeared from my hand. By the time I found it, frantically clawing around in the sand for the mike cord, Miss High Octane—as we called her among ourselves—was soaked and shivering back on the beach.

The audience never did know what had happened, and I had no intention of explaining it. I saw my thousand a week ebbing with the tide, and I went home that night with sand in my teeth and despair in my heart.

The next day I got the expected summons from the J. Walter

Thompson office, and my friend Danny Danker had the un-happy assignment of telling me the grim news. He said the president of the Shell Oil Company, who had been on a Euro-pean vacation when my contract was signed, had come home and listened with horror to the playbacks of my first two shows. He had wanted Leopold Stokowski and the Philadelphia Orchestra, not some clown tripping over drunks and logs, and he said: "Cancel Linkletter."

I knew I was not the world's greatest radio attraction, but at the same time I was peeved with what I thought was a stodgy and inconsistent attitude. I pointed out to the assembled lawyers, who had come there with briefcases full of loopholes, that the oil company billboards were at that moment covered by a funny William Steig cartoon which showed motorists heading for an outhouse behind a service station. Surely this was more undignified than a bathing beauty splashing in the surf—I said.

I was trying to salvage the eleven thousand dollars still due on my contract, of course, but my arguments were useless. The agency people delicately suggested that they had many other shows, and that if I didn't play rough they would reward me for my good sportsmanship. So I signed an agreement— they just happened to have it all made up—to settle my contract for fifteen hundred dollars. I left there with my confidence shaved down to a shadow, but when I got home Lois reported an urgent phone call from the ad agency. "They want you to come right down to the office," she said. *Well*, I thought, *they didn't waste any time getting me another show.*

I drove back to downtown Hollywood, and I found the entire J. Walter Thompson high command in a wild-eyed stew. They had made a staggering error in the release I signed, agreeing to settle my contract—not for fifteen hundred dollars —but for $150,000. They showed me how a typist had made the mistake and they conceded that not one of the signing executives had noticed the wrong amount. I was an unknown quantity in Hollywood, and they must have had a searing moment of panic, wondering what I would do about it. I kidded them a little, but I signed a new release that took them off the hook. Twice in one day I had been a good guy. I was sure my friendliness would pay off, and that they would phone me. And I was right. They did call—seven years later.

iii

I may be inconsistent when I say that the loss of eleven thousand dollars was not nearly as crushing to me as the summary dismissal by a sponsor. But I was not accustomed to being associated with a flop, and in a gossipy milieu such as Hollywood the word soon gets around that a performer is a jinx, or a dud, and the agencies suddenly begin to cool off.

Nevertheless, I had to keep going. I knew that network radio was for me and that the big money was in Hollywood and nowhere else.

Optimism doesn't pay the grocery bill, of course, and I was glad that I had not completely severed my connections in San Francisco. I was flying north once a week to do the "Who's Dancing Tonight?" show for the Samuels jewelry firm, and this ace-in-the-hole was paying the overhead. On weekdays I was a tireless master of ceremonies, and I was available for openings at supermarkets, bowling alleys, movie theaters and other places the big names wouldn't touch at any price.

I went to scores of small towns in the Southern California area where crowds gathered for some special event, and quite often I was at the same speaker's table, or up on a decorated stand, with a young lawyer who was just learning the fundamental techniques of politics. This young man was not naturally an extrovert, and I could see that crowd handling and public speaking put him under great strain.

"Art," he said to me one evening, "I've never seen you flustered with an audience. It seems so easy for you. How do you do it?"

"Whenever I'm nervous or apprehensive about a crowd that looks formidable," I said, "I remember some old-fashioned advice I first heard when I was at school in San Diego. I look down at the audience, and I imagine they are all sitting there in their underwear. The mental picture seems so ludicrous that I lose all fear."

He laughed and said: "I'll have to try that."

My politician friend is Richard M. Nixon, and when I see him on television—poised, smooth and forceful—I cannot help wondering whether, in his mind's eye, the people are all sitting there in their undies.

iv

A month or so after the Shell fiasco, the Los Angeles *Times* asked me to conduct a news and variety show called "Who, What, Where and Why." The show was a promotion gimmick, and the sponsor was a potent force in the Los Angeles area. But someone should have asked "When?" We had an excellent time slot, but along came Bob Hope with a top-rated national show and we were squeezed out of our spot. The program was canceled, and for the third time in a few short weeks I found myself yanked off the air.

Those were depressing days, and my big dream was suddenly a nightmare.

I told myself that these failures were not really my fault, and I believed it. Every performer I knew in Hollywood had been on the skids at one time or another, often through circumstances beyond his control, and had made it to the top. I could too. During this bleak period, when I was down on one knee taking the count and shaking the numbness out of my brain, I was making notes on new program ideas.

One listless afternoon—and how the bills were piling up at home—I went to see a new-found friend named John Guedel. John was a writer and producer who had contributed his pixie talents to the writing of Hal Roach comedies, and who at that moment wrote and owned a successful radio show called "Pull Over, Neighbor." He knew it was successful because it had been on the air two years, and paid him seventy-five dollars a week.

John and I went to lunch at the Brown Derby on Vine Street —this is not exactly a drive-in hot dog stand—and we sat in a booth for a couple of hours. This was part of the Hollywood routine. You sat at the Derby, whether you were a potential starlet with a forty-two-inch bust or a writer with a plot, and you took phone calls at the table, or had yourself paged. There were always important producers and directors in adjoining booths, and as they gulped down vitamins or soda bicarb or ulcer pills they might hear your name and suddenly tap you for immortality. But it never happens that way, of course.

While John and I were toying with the bread crumbs, I mentioned that I had an idea for a show to be called "Meet Yourself." This was to be an entertaining study of human behavior, based on a file of case histories I had borrowed from a San Francisco psychologist.

"That's odd," John said. "I've been talking to a psychology professor at the University of California, and going through his files. We were going to do a behavior show too, and call it 'People Are Funny.'"

We stopped doodling with the crumbs and blinked at each other like blind men who have suddenly regained their sight. "C'mon," John said. We hurried to his office, half a block away, and spent hectic hours shaping a rough format. The following day, killing time in a dentist's office, John read a small item in *Variety* which said that the Brown & Williamson Tobacco Company was looking for a summer replacement. Their current program, "Sergeant Quirt and Captain Flagg," was taking a licking in the ratings. Moreover, with the United States mobilizing and the dreadful certainty of eventual war, the Government was frowning on a plot that featured rowdy dialogue between an officer and a non-com.

John promptly forgot the hole in his tooth and phoned me with the challenging news.

We worked far into the night, blocking out the show on paper, and cut an audition record the next morning. It cost us fifteen dollars each—as I recall that was all the cash we could spare at the time—and we shipped it airmail to the Chicago ad agency handling the tobacco account. Two days later, we got a phone call that had us whooping and jumping around like a couple of Sweepstakes winners.

"We'll buy the show," the agency man said, "but we've never heard of this fellow Art Linkletter. Get a big name who can work with him."

John had frequently worked with Art Baker, who was a seasoned pro even then, and the agency agreed to engage him as co-emcee. We would have hired King Kong to get the show on the air, and People Are Funny made its debut, coast to coast, in June, 1941. It was essentially a slapstick show—we had decided the serious psychological approach lacked appeal—and we soon discovered that when it comes to natural humor there is nothing like people. I have since written profound essays and given erudite talks about the secret of People Are Funny. Actually there was nothing mysterious about it at all. Hundreds of people seem to enjoy making themselves look silly; millions of others get hysterical watching ordinary men and women go through these antics. This was not slick, professional humor. This was pure corn.

It took only one show to prove the thesis. I had a volunteer contestant on the stage and was ad libbing questions. Thinking about baseball, I said: "In what sport is the squeeze play used?"

"Post office," he said without a smile.

When the laughter subsided, I asked: "And what would you call your wife, who has stood by you all these years so faithfully? Old what?"

"Old Ironsides," he said.

When I heard the joyous yelps from the audience, I knew we would never have to pay a thousand a week for skilled gag writers. No pro could ever match the spontaneous quips from our home-grown wits who, in most cases, had no idea their remarks were funny.

When People Are Funny was in its fourth week, and surprising the experts with its rapid climb, Art Baker asked me to have dinner with him. We went to the Derby and Baker casually said: "Art, it isn't working out."

"What isn't working out?"

"One of us has got to go," he said. "There can't be two emcees on the show."

I was so surprised that I absent-mindedly reached for the ketchup bottle to put some on my steak.

"You really mean that?" I asked.

"I certainly do," he said.

I went back to the office of John Guedel Productions, in which I now had a solid stake, and told John about my unpalatable dinner. We talked it out, and finally told Baker that we were sorry to see him go, but if that was what he wanted we would wish him luck and find another man. You cannot imagine my consternation when, phoning the agency people in Chicago to discuss the change, we were bluntly told to forget it. They wanted Art Baker—not an unknown like me. I fought their definition of anonymity, knowing that my name had been heard around the country through three world fairs, but they wouldn't back down. It was Baker—or else.

John and I took the ultimatum with dismay. We owned the show and we had staked our future on it. But at that point neither of us had the money or the nerve to risk a showdown. I was squeezed out of my own show, and it was a galling dose to take.

I was all through. This was the last and the worst of the shock waves and I couldn't take any more. I knew I would have to go back to San Francisco and start all over.

I walked out of Guedel's office and stood on the corner of Vine Street, looking at the long chain of shimmering lights on Hollywood Boulevard. A radio transmitting tower pierced the dark stretch of sky high above the busy street, lofty, beyond reach, and it seemed to be a symbol of my defeat. There were people passing by me, hurrying home, but I might as well have been on a raft far out at sea. I was terribly alone.

I have never forgotten that intersection at Hollywood and Vine, and by a curious coincidence I was standing at the very spot some years later when I saw a man leaning against a building and glumly gazing at the passing stream. He had a cap pulled down over his eyes, but I recognized him and spoke to him.

"Hello, Art," he said huskily.

"You in trouble?" I asked.

"Yeah," he said. "This town has me beat and I'm going back to New York where I came from."

So I told him my story—how I stood on that corner years before, a self-confessed failure with my big chance down the drain, and how I made the decision to quit Hollywood. "It was perhaps the best move I ever made," I said, "and I'm sure it will be for you." We shook hands and he ambled away. He did go back to New York, and within a year he had become one of the great comedians in television. His name is Jackie Gleason.

11. The Past Catches Up

> *On an early People Are Funny show I was
> interviewing an eighteen-year-old secretary and I
> posed this question: "If you had two apples, one
> small and brown, the other large and shiny, which
> one would you give to your best friend?"*
>
> *"The large and shiny one," she said without
> hesitation.*
>
> *"Why?" I asked.*
>
> *"Because I don't like apples," she said.*

IN THE FALL of 1941 I would have traded all the large and shiny
apples in San Francisco for one small, brown one in Hollywood.

In my business I am often thought of as a carefree, confident
man who is almost never thrown for a loss, either by a thought-
less crack from some troublemaker on my show, or by some
personal setback. But I was far from happy and confident when
I submissively crawled back to San Francisco. Our friends had
sent us southward with whistles and flags flying—we had
barely unpacked some of our going-away gifts—and here we
were back at the old stand. Local boy doesn't make good.

My surrender at the time was so complete that Lois and I
bought a rather large house in the St. Francis Woods district
of San Francisco, and settled down there as though it would
be a permanent base.

There are residents of San Francisco, still living, who survived the Linkletter barrage of the Forties, and who swear I was on all three networks and half a dozen independent stations day and night. This is only a mild exaggeration. I was still doing my "Who's Dancing Tonight?" show from the downtown hotels. I had a daily disk jockey show on KSFO and a KGO program for the famous Gump's store called "Gallery of Celebrities," a second program from KGO titled "Search for a Genius," and I was conducting "Spell for Dough," a harmless little quiz show at the Claremont Hotel in Berkeley, home of the University of California.

In between the radio programs, I was rocketing in every direction as a roving master of ceremonies. "Art was willing," my friend Clyde Vandeburg says. "He would have emceed a knitting bee at the Old Ladies' Home if it meant getting his name around." This is a fair analysis, as my scrapbook shows. Among other events, I emceed high school dances in Lafayette, on the east side of San Francisco Bay, and in Aptos, eighty miles or so south on Santa Cruz Bay. I worked a show in Woodland, in a farm area to the north, and I handled the mike at the Rice Bowl Festival in San Francisco's Chinatown. The high intellectual level of these personal appearances can be measured by one typical activity at the Chinatown Festival. For charity I auctioned off a mystery gift to Mr. Charlie Low, the shrewd and penny-wise owner of a lavish nightclub called The Forbidden City. Charlie eagerly bid thirty-five dollars for the beribboned box which, when he got it open, contained one stale peanut.

Father Linkletter sent me a brief note once, when I was on this treadmill, and quoted the line from the Bible which says: "Much learning doth make thee mad." It was his way of suggesting that perhaps I was scattering my talents and not sticking to one program or locale. I was learning, to be sure, but rather than making me mad it was teaching me basic facts about people that I stored away for future use.

One such lesson—and I remember it as the most embarrassing and amateurish show I ever did—came when I agreed to take a troupe of third-rate dancers and singers to entertain GI's at Fort Ord, on the Monterey coast 125 miles south of San Francisco. The nation was on the march, and the men at Fort Ord were not ordinary soldiers. They were expert mechanics and engineers who had given up well-paying jobs all over the country to assemble army tanks.

I didn't know about them, of course, but perhaps I wouldn't have done it differently anyway.

In any case, I had had no rehearsals, and I thought I could do the show off the cuff. Worst of all, I arrived at this hot and dusty army camp in cream colored flannels and a flashy sports jacket, and I had wisecracks to match. I knew I was dead the moment I looked down at those grimy, tired men, and for the first time in my life, as this atrocious show unfolded, I heard the chilling sound of boos.

I deserved what I got that day.

Driving home, I was ashamed of the poor job I had done and remorseful about the natty civilian clothes I had worn in front of men in uniform who had made such a personal sacrifice. Also, I learned the lesson every Boy Scout knows—be prepared! I never again went out on an emcee job without knowing what kind of an audience I would face, and what kind of material to use.

These hit-and-run trips—many were appearances at hospitals and army camps—were a primer for me in the handling of off-beat audiences. I thought I had just about run through the catalogue at the fairs in San Diego, Dallas and San Francisco, but I picked up some new rules which were to be valuable in later years.

I have often heard people criticize an emcee for what they claimed were cruel remarks to handicapped men and women.

I found out that cruelty is a two-way street. What may sound callous to the average man has a quite different effect on a subject who has some marked physical drawback. I went to a hospital at Pearl Harbor, shortly after the Japanese attack, and entertained in a ward jammed with wounded men. There was one young fellow in the front row who had lost both arms, and when I looked at him my heart sank. But instead of making some inane sentimental remark, I singled him out and said: "Well, sailor, you're not going to be much use to me. If there's anything a performer likes it's applause. The least you can do is whistle."

There were probably people in that ward who thought I had made a terribly heartless remark. But during the show, that boy, unable to clap, whistled and yelled louder than all the rest, and as I was leaving he stopped me at the door.

"Thanks for not pitying me, Art," he said, eyes shining. "You gave me what I needed."

I had a similar experience at the leper colony on the island of Molokai in Hawaii. My audience there consisted of sixty-five men and women who, hopelessly ill, were doomed to spend their entire lives on this distant island. I knew they would not want sympathy and I opened the show by saying: "You will not be surprised to hear that we are going to have a drawing here for you, and the winner gets a free trip to New York to see all the shows." This was such a ludicrous idea to these imprisoned souls that they literally doubled up with laughter, and the program turned into one of the happiest shows I have ever done.

There was one other show during this period that vividly comes to life in my memory.

I had been invited to visit a certain penitentiary and I was to entertain several thousand men gathered in the huge mess hall. Among the men given special dispensation that day was—well . . . let's call him Johnny Q., a tough stick-up artist who had a long record of escape attempts there and in other prisons.

Johnny was pointed out to me before I came on stage, and I was warned that he was a mean, loud-mouthed inmate who would most certainly needle me in order to attract the attention of other prisoners.

As I started my show I looked down over the footlights and said: "Well . . . I see Johnny Q. is with us today. I didn't think he'd be around."

I let that thought penetrate a moment, and I could see him scowling. "The fact is," I said, "I was coming through the yard this afternoon, and I saw Johnny Q. running alongside the wall with a long stick in his hand. Yes—he heard there's going to be a track meet here tomorrow—and he's going to enter the pole vault."

There was a tremendous explosion of laughter and I thought the guard on the catwalk overhead would fall off his perch. Johnny Q. grimaced, then began to smile, and in a moment he was shaking with laughter, too. They'd never had a pole vault at the prison track meets, of course, but the idea must have appealed to Johnny Q. He went over the wall with a crude ladder one dark night, and for all I know he may be laughing about it yet.

ii

Pearl Harbor Day changed the face of the earth. And, to a degree that was important only to me, it completely re-shaped my personal and professional life.

With the nation at war, and millions of men training in

camps from coast to coast, the men and women of the entertainment world found themselves with a triple responsibility. They not only had to keep up their regular bookings, but they were called on to perform for government agencies broadcasting both propaganda and entertainment overseas, and in their spare time they took their shows to the big army, navy and marine training centers.

In San Francisco, along with my commercial programs, I began working on the short-wave broadcasts by the Office of War Information, and I shuttled from OWI to Nelson Rockefeller's Committee of Inter-American Affairs, which was beaming powerful transmitters to Latin-American nations. I was also radio program director for the vast Kaiser shipyards in the port of Richmond, on the east rim of San Francisco Bay.

To Nelson Rockefeller, I was merely a name and number during those tense months, and I did not meet him. It was only recently, some eighteen years later, that I had a chance to introduce myself and remind him that he was my wartime boss. We were at the head table at an elaborate Republican Party dinner in Syracuse, and the toastmaster asked me to say a few words.

I have always enjoyed kidding celebrities. I deliberately test their ability to take it, and when anyone asks me to say a few words I am like Niagara Falls—impossible to shut off. Anyway, I looked down at Nelson Rockefeller, who was now Governor of New York, and I told the audience that I took orders from him during the war. "I've only been in this state a few days," I said, "but I have heard many comments about the kind of job Governor Rockefeller is doing here. I would be happy to repeat those comments, but I can't. There are ladies present." It was a harmless little spoof—and not too original— but I was relieved to see the Governor chuckling along with everyone else.

At the Richmond shipyard, I was not Christopher Marlowe's

"face that launched a thousand ships," but I was at the microphone, describing every detail, when at least a hundred vessels
slid down the ways. There, too, I was just another employee
and though Henry Kaiser often saw me at the microphone we
had no social contact. I was awestruck then by Kaiser's well-
spring of energy and imagination—he was already sixty years
old—and as the years went on, with me as a one-man admiration
society, we became close personal friends.

I have never been known as a name dropper, but it gave
me a great sense of satisfaction to be in the inner sanctum, so
to speak, with Henry Kaiser. But it is curious how little we
know of a man we have seen hundreds of times. I had talked
with him often, dined with him, been a house guest at his
Hawaiian estate. But one day, at his Lake Tahoe summer home
in California, I made a wry discovery.

We were playing volleyball, and among the participants
were the Governor of California, Goodwin Knight, and my
old friend Bob Cummings. It was all very gay and informal,
but I suddenly became aware of the fact that every man and
woman there—including Mrs. Kaiser—addressed the host as
"Mr. Kaiser." He had called me Art for years, and I always
called him Henry.

When the game broke up, Kaiser and I walked alone to
the lakeshore. "I've just noticed that everyone calls you Mr.
Kaiser," I said. "Do you mind my calling you Henry? I've been
doing it for years, but now I see that I am the exception."

He gazed at me with those remarkable eyes of his, and I
suddenly regretted my question. "No," he said, "I have no
objection. Other people call me Mr. Kaiser, I think, in an
affectionate sort of way, using the word Mister like a title.
The way some people are called Colonel or Judge."

It was a forthright and logical explanation, but I had a strange
sense of uneasiness about it. Since then I have called him

Henry less and less, and when I do it, it is with an uneasy feeling of guilt. Perhaps I don't know him at all. Matter of fact, he may be thinking up a new name for me. Several years ago, he phoned from Hawaii and asked me whether the Kaiser interests should sponsor a new and untried television show called "Maverick," starring an unknown named James Garner over ABC.

"Certainly not," I said. "There are already a jillion Westerns on the air, and in the proposed time slot you'll be bucking three champions—Ed Sullivan, Steve Allen and Jack Benny."

Kaiser promptly signed up the show. "Maverick" not only shot up to the top with fabulous ratings, but it seriously crippled the opposition. Henry—I mean Mr. Kaiser—graciously remained silent but, needless to say, he never again asked me for advice about a new television show.

iii

The war had been raging six or seven months when I suddenly realized that I was standing on the rim of a cliff and that inevitably someone would push me over.

My friends in San Francisco knew me as a happy, successful young man of thirty with a lovely wife and two fine children. I was earning perhaps seventy-five thousand dollars a year. I had an exceptionally nice home on Francisco Way, though I was seeing very little of it, and my name was as well known around town as that of Mayor Angelo Rossi or any other public figure. Within the boundaries of my local radio world, I had climbed as high as I could go.

But I was living a fraud.

I am sure there were servicemen at my many camp shows who could see that I was young and obviously healthy, and who undoubtedly wondered how I had escaped the draft.

When I was asked about it—and occasionally some of the questions were blunt—I simply told the truth, that I had been deferred because of my work on the government information and propaganda programs. But it was not quite the whole story. The truth was that I was not an American citizen. I was a Canadian and therefore, in a technical sense, I was an alien. I was not only an alien, but I was pretending to be an American citizen, and during wartime this was a dangerous and foolish masquerade.

In the entertainment business, and I am no exception, most performers hire clever press agents to extol their virtues and keep their name and face alive. If a press agent is on the ball, the public usually knows all about a star's legal love life, where he dines, who curls his hair and tailors his clothes and other bits of personal information which—we keep telling ourselves —make us more human to the people who watch our shows.

But the stars also pay press agents to keep unpleasant news out of the papers. Millions are spent to create a box office image, and that image must be protected at any cost. I do not think this is quite honest. But I cannot cast the first stone because there are chapters in my life which, like the untold story of my real parents, have been carefully hidden away in closets.

There were almost no personal friends in San Francisco who knew the secret of my nationality.

I simply did not talk about it. But the irony was that any-one who cared to investigate—I never suspected that people actually were checking up on me—would have come across newspaper clippings or other documents which mentioned the fact that I had been born in Moose Jaw in Canada. At San

Diego State College there were files which contained all the information about my foreign birth and my adoption by John and Mary Linkletter.

But now it was wartime, and in my daily work I was acutely conscious of the fact that people's passions were far more inflammable than in peacetime. Few of them stopped to differentiate between "alien" and "enemy alien." Gossip about spies in the Bay area was as potentially deadly as a detonating cap. People were irrational and blind about many things.

I was not only vulnerable, but I was terribly afraid. I thought of my confidential work at the powerful radio stations whose messages reached around the world, and I could almost hear some crackpot, afire with patriotic zeal, pointing an accusing finger at me and branding me a spy.

So it was fear that drove me to cover.

When the subject came up in publicity interviews, I now said that I had been born in Lowell, Massachusetts. I filled out identity card applications at Stations KWID and KSFO—the government-controlled propaganda outlets—and said I was an American citizen. I voted in an election and used the same white lie. In the loneliness of the night, I kept telling myself that I was not doing wrong. I thought that I might be barred from the short-wave stations if the truth were known. I had an even more dreadful thought—the chance that I might be deported.

On September 29, 1942, not knowing where else to turn, I went to the naturalization bureau of the United States Immigration Service.

I thought it was a wise move. If I applied for American citizenship as I had always intended, my conscience would be clear. I should have done it years before, but like many another man, I had stalled and kept this item at the bottom of the duty pile. Now here I was, trying to put out the fire with a water pistol. The immigration people were sympathetic and polite, and they gave me the proper forms to fill out. Among other grave errors, I stated I had never been out of the United States —completely overlooking the trip I had made to South America with Denver Fox. Anyway, I raced through the forms, and left the office with a great sense of relief. I was on my way to a new life as Art Linkletter, American citizen.

Then, on a chilly December day, a little more than two months after my visit to the Immigration office, the bottom fell out of my world.

I was walking down the slight grade of Powell Street, near the St. Francis Hotel on Union Square, when my eyes swept over a newspaper rack on the corner and the headline jumped up and hit me. It read: ART LINKLETTER INDICTED.

I find myself unable to describe the impact of those big black letters. The sun was shining low in the morning sky, but I didn't see it. There were people flowing in the sidewalk current and the cable car was clacking along in its little slot. But I heard no sound. I only know that for a moment there were invisible hands at my throat. I snatched up a copy of the paper without paying for it, ran around the corner and found refuge in a dark corner of an office building lobby.

I held the paper in front of my face because I did not want to be recognized by anyone at this devastating moment. I read the story. It could not have been more shocking. I had been indicted by the Federal Grand Jury in San Francisco for falsely claiming to be an American citizen. The government accused me of lying about my birthplace, of illegally voting in an election, and of falsely stating that I had never been out of the United States. The account further reported that I had not yet been arrested, but that bail had been set at twenty-five hundred dollars.

In such crises your mind can easily run off the track and skitter around in wild little circles.

I am not a man who panics easily. But at that moment, on the morning of December 8, there was no question but that I was in a panic.

I had never been arrested or accused of a crime, but now I could hear cell doors slamming shut. I could hear the buzzing of angry gossip. I could hear myself being denounced on street corners and in the press. I could see the vicious letters spewing into the mail room at the studios. I knew my radio career was done. I was afraid. I slunk out of the lobby, wishing I had a hat to pull down over my eyes, and I almost ran to the office of my lawyer, William A. "Bill" O'Brien, momentarily expecting the touch of a heavy hand.

"Well, Art," O'Brien said when I showed him the paper, "what's the answer?"

"There isn't any answer, Bill," I said. "It's true."

"All of it?"

"All of it."

"Tell me about it."

So I told him. Among other things I said I had foolishly assumed that the Linkletters had become naturalized citizens at some point during those early years, and that therefore I automatically had become a citizen, too. But even as I groped for some excuse, however slim, I knew in my heart that this was an evasion. Like the reporter who didn't check his facts because he was afraid he wouldn't have a story, I had never discussed the problem with Father Linkletter. I knew what the answer would be.

O'Brien gloomily agreed that I had no alibi, but he was not quite ready to quit.

"We might beat it with a jury, Art," he said. "I feel sure there would be twelve people who would give you a fair hearing and who would be convinced that you had no criminal intent."

"I can't do it, Bill," I said.

"Why not?"

"Because it would involve my real parents. The Kellys would be brought out here to testify, and the publicity would be murder."

"In that case," O'Brien said, "there isn't much left but *nolo contendere*."

"What's that?"

"It's a plea which doesn't admit guilt, but which in effect says you have no defense."

"Okay. Whatever you say."

O'Brien phoned the office of the United States Marshal, and said he would surrender me in the morning. We went through the necessary formalities, posted the bail and asked for an early date in court. Only a man who has faced the bursting stars of flashlight bulbs and the black exposure in print can understand the shame I felt. It was like standing naked before a mocking crowd, with no place to hide. It was nightmare enough to know that conviction could mean five years in prison and a five thousand dollar fine. There had been four similar indictments of other men; each had pleaded guilty and each was fined and sent to a Federal penitentiary for a year and a day.

But the deepest wound of all was the damage to my name.

In my profession everyone is name-conscious. The measure of success in show business is not always how much money you make, but whether your name is instantly recognized by the average radio, television or movie fan, and what people are saying. The building of a name often takes years, and great personal sacrifices are the rule rather than the exception. But scandal can swiftly wipe your name into oblivion—as a sponge sweeps across a slate—and usually the most desperate and heroic first aid can not bring it back.

And this was where I stood in January of 1943, when the

case was set for hearing. The eraser was poised, the future was bleak for Lois and me.

Bill O'Brien and I went early to the court of Federal Judge Michael J. Roche, and few of my friends would have recognized the once blithe and breezy Art Linkletter who could handle any situation in a studio. I knew I was finished. I had put my business affairs in order, and I was ready to take my punishment. I watched Judge Roche for some clue that might suggest what sort of mood he was in, and as I waited there was a prisoner standing before the bench, head bowed.

Judge Roche looked down, rattled some papers and said coldly: "Twenty years."

My stomach flipped, and when my case was called O'Brien pleaded me guilty and asked for probation. One week later—and a more miserable seven days I have never known—I went back to the same court for sentencing and a report on the probation request.

"It strikes me, Mr. Linkletter," Judge Roche said, "that a man with your capacity should not have done this thing. I can't understand your disregard for the law."

"Your honor," I said—and in my more than one hundred and fifty thousand broadcasts I have never put so much of my heart into words—"I have no disrespect for the law. It was an error of judgment. It was an error I regret and will continue to regret. I have suffered many weeks of anguish, and I wish to God I had never done these things."

Judge Roche nodded, but he was still frowning. "Perhaps your success made you feel that it was not necessary for you to obey the law," he said.

"I have never had such thoughts, your honor," I said. "In my heart I have never known anything but America and Americanism. The word alien seems strange to me."

"If I were to excuse you, Mr. Linkletter," the jurist continued—and by this time I was bracing myself—"it would set a precedent. Every weak-minded person in the community would think that his own interpretation of the law would be sufficient. It is not a case for probation. Probation denied."

The newspaper accounts of the hearing—which I have before me—reported that "Linkletter and his attorney paled." I am sure we did. I heard O'Brien catch his breath when he heard the word "denied," and I know the blood drained from my face.

"I fine you five hundred dollars," Judge Roche said. "I am extending to you the charity of this country in this fine. The alternative is six months in the county jail."

Perhaps Judge Roche noticed my agitation because for a moment the sternness faded from his eyes. "Mr. Linkletter," he said in a kindlier tone, "I am convinced you have the makings of a good citizen, and for that reason I am denying probation so this matter can be cleared up as quickly as possible, and you will not have a long probationary period delaying your application for American citizenship. Case closed."

I have long since proudly become an American citizen, but I have never forgotten that morning seventeen years ago. I learned how the courts jealously guard certain basic rights you have or don't have as a citizen of the United States. I also learned, I hope, that there are problems in life that can't be solved by glib talk alone, or by sticking them out of sight in some dusty niche. And I am certain, looking back now, that I found a new meaning for the word maturity that morning when Judge Roche generously gave me another chance.

12. Try "Dear Abby" Instead

Some years ago I contracted a bad case of laryngitis, and my doctor advised me to dash into a hospital near the studio every day and get a shot of penicillin.

I followed his orders for five days, and each morning a pretty young nurse silently and efficiently jabbed my stern with a needle. Finally I said: "Miss, you haven't said a thing about my House Party show. Don't you ever listen to it?"

"Yes, I do," she said. "But I like to have a mental picture of the performer. The trouble with you is that you run in and out of here so fast every day that when I hear your show I can't visualize your face."

I NATURALLY WONDERED, when I was found guilty by Judge Roche, what sort of mental picture my radio listeners would have of me. I hoped they would not think of me as the part where nurses put the needle.

Some of my friends and business advisors were worried, and at least one suggested that it might have been better, from a public relations viewpoint, if I had been penalized more severely. In my heart though, I felt that no prison term could possibly be more punitive than my profound remorse and public humiliation. Fortunately, as one reporter friend said: "There is nothing as dead as yesterday's newspaper," and I was grateful for the fact that the press and the public quickly forgot the Linkletter case.

However, knowing something about the fickleness of mankind, I anticipated losing some of my shows.

There was at least one advertising agency man for whom I worked who had some doubts about my future value to his client. He telephoned Jay Haight, then director of sales promotion for my main sponsor, the Albert S. Samuels Company, and wanted to know what he thought about the unpleasant publicity. Haight, for whom I had been doing my "Who's Dancing Tonight?" show, quickly replied: "Art is okay with us, and he's going to stay." The ad man accepted that verdict, and I continued doing his program, too.

Luckily, Father and Mother Linkletter knew nothing about my troubles.

They were still living in the upstairs apartment on East Second Street in Pomona, and clinging to the habits of a lifetime. They rarely read the newspapers, and almost never went beyond the periphery of their insular little world. I remembered that Mother Linkletter had always dreamed of owning her own home, and on a visit to Pomona I offered to buy them a small house in Pomona or Los Angeles, or anywhere else they might want to live.

They talked it over eagerly for two or three days, then reluctantly concluded the change would be too much. There was security and comfort in their two rooms, and Mother wisely felt that the housekeeping chores of a larger home would demand more energy than she had. So I had their apartment repapered and painted, and gave them a piano and television set. They wanted nothing more.

In 1944, when Father was eighty-three years old, he suffered the first serious illness of his life. He was stricken with pneumonia, and he fussed and fretted because he had to stay in bed. He always had remarkable physical strength, and I could almost see him shaking his fist at the four walls that held him and angrily telling the doctors that no puny virus could lick him. But now the old vigor was gone, and the fight was lost. He died quietly in his sleep, an isolated man who had never quite caught up with the times.

I never doubted that he loved me, in his own unfathomable way. But I think I was little more than an image he had built into his mind. *Dear Artie,* as he had said and written so many times. And that's how it was to the end.

Often at the death of a loved one, we sorrow at the blows life has dealt him, at his frustrated dreams, his unreached goals, and we wish he might have had a second chance. But I could feel none of these regrets for Father Linkletter. He had been a preacher and a humble cobbler whose happiness in life was doing his work well. He never found reason to stop loving his fellow man, or to stop helping him. He had so often shown us the power of simple goodness, and at all times he had been sustained by complete confidence in the justness of his God. He would not have altered the course of his life in the slightest degree.

And so I could not grieve for him.

I could only know that I was a better man for what he gave, and that I would be less so with him gone. When I look at our marriage certificate and remember the wedding he missed, and re-read his scribbled letter to Lois, I hope I will always be "Dear Artie" to him—wherever he may be.

ii

During the busy months when I was buzzing San Francisco radio like an elusive mosquito on a hot summer's night, I stole time on weekends to write special material for the People Are Funny show in Hollywood.

I wrote stunts, skits and gags for Art Baker, the man who didn't want me on the same stage with him, and I was rewarded by seeing the show go into a steady climb. When *Variety* began listing People Are Funny in the top twenty nationally, I felt the time had come to regain my place. Hollywood no longer held any terrors for me. I had gone through the blood bath there the first time, and in San Francisco I had survived two or three wild skirmishes that could have finished my career. So I was ready for a second invasion of the big time, and no matter what happened I knew I would not be hurt again.

John Guedel dropped Art Baker and reinstated me as master of ceremonies for our show. Unhappily, Baker disregarded the fact that John and I created and owned the program. In effect he said we had no right to run our own show, and in a protest suit filed with the American Federation of Radio Artists, he said we should have given him a permanent contract. The AFRA three-man arbitration committee—including the man Baker personally chose to represent him—was unanimous in ruling against him, and he probably has never forgotten it. I regret there was so much bitterness in this affair, but there can certainly be no argument about my right to guide my own show.

Being familiar with the high mortality rate of Hollywood radio shows, I think John and I were at first inclined to be cautious about the success of People Are Funny.

I recall that John used to bring his lunch in a paper bag and eat it at his desk, and I kidded him about it until he finally decided he could afford to go to the Derby once in a while. We also took out fifty thousand dollar insurance policies on each other's life, and there was some good-natured ribbing about that. When I got into an airplane to go to San Francisco or anywhere else, John would rub his hands and say: "This time you crash—maybe." I, on the other hand, could always bring him out of the blues by pointing to the open window, high above Vine Street, and saying: "Go ahead, John, jump! Just think—fifty thousand for me."

Our mutual prudence soon disappeared, though, when we were both touched by another Hollywood miracle.

John took a trip to New York and—between the new shows, lunch at Twenty-One and the inevitable cocktail parties—he sandwiched in a visit with the radio director for the Young & Rubicam agency.

"What's new?" John said casually.

"Oh, not much," the agency man replied.

"Can't sell you anything today?"

"Well . . . if you happen to have a show that'll run a half hour five days a week we might talk about it."

Guedel, who can tell wonderful lies when he is in the mood, replied: "It so happens we have exactly what you want. I'll bring it in tomorrow."

He telephoned me in Hollywood that evening, and after batting ideas around for half an hour or so, we came up with the format for the House Party show. General Electric bought the package the next day for five thousand dollars a week, and gave us a five-year contract on the full CBS network. I had no idea, of course, that this deceptively simple framework would survive more than fifteen years on radio and television, but there was soon evidence that I had drilled into an inexhaustible lode when I started working with children.

One of my first guests was a little six-year-old girl, golden-haired, eyes like the morning sky. "You have the prettiest dimples," I said. "I guess God gave you those."

"No," she replied. "Mommy says I got them from the ice man."

The little girl's mother looked around wildly for refuge, but the audience went into a spasm of laughter. I started collecting these blunders and quips and eventually, as delirious book dealers everywhere now know, wrapped them all up in a best-selling volume called "Kids Say the Darndest Things."

iii

With two successful network shows, and our income more or less guaranteed by long-term contracts, Lois and I bought a large and comfortable house on a side street half a block off the glittering Sunset Strip.

I thought I knew something about the quixotic life in Hollywood. I had seen fleeting glimpses of it on my first stay when I was commuting by air for some of my shows. But I soon realized that I had only the tourist's view, and that the perspective of the natives was quite different.

When I was living in San Francisco, for instance, I had strong and belligerent feelings about celebrities who had unlisted telephone numbers. From time to time, traveling south for a weekend, I tried calling some of the stars I had interviewed in San Francisco, and when I got the unlisted number run-around I was almost angry enough to jerk out the wires. *This is ridiculous*, I said to myself. *Just because you have fame and money it doesn't entitle you to be a snob.* Accordingly, when we got a telephone for our new house I had the number listed in the phone book.

Presently I was on the air five days a week, my picture was appearing in the newspapers, and the fan magazines were plugging my shows. Then it began. The Mormons fighting off the locusts had nothing on me. The phone jangled all day and half the night with callers crying: *Send me money . . . Get me out of jail . . . I desperately need a job . . . Lift the mortgage on our house . . . My old mother is dying and I can't pay for the funeral . . . I've got an idea and we'll both get rich.*

Drunks were calling me at midnight from bars in Omaha or New Orleans or Boston. Finally, when a violent anti-Linkletter listener—and there are some here and there—phoned me with the most scorching cussing I have ever heard, I yelled to the phone company for help. They gave me an unlisted number, and there was peace in the house once more.

By this time—with the birth of our second son, Robert—there were five in our family and the increase in the population raised certain problems.

Our furniture, among other things around the house, was beginning to look as though it had spent a rough summer at a YMCA camp. We had hauled it back and forth from Los Angeles to San Francisco, and from house to house, and it was beyond salvage. So Lois went to one of the fashionable stores in Los Angeles and bought some new furniture that was sturdy enough to withstand a stampede by the Marx brothers—whom we had just met—or a thundering herd of small boys who would soon be headquartering there.

We were not home when the furniture store delivery truck arrived, and with no check forthcoming the driver refused to leave it. I phoned the store immediately, and indignantly protested that my credit was good enough in San Francisco, and it ought to be good in Hollywood. After all, I said with as much modesty as I could muster, I was a radio star with two nationally rated shows, and there were no bill collectors parked outside my door. The store people apologized and said they would send a vice president to see me.

He rang the doorbell presently—urbane, cool and polite—and we sat down on our old beat-up sofa.

"Mr. Linkletter," he said, taking one haughty glance around the room, "please let me give you the facts of life."

"Biology?" I snapped.

"No," he said stiffly. "Economics. Now you have a lovely and expensive house here. Big swimming pool, garden, built-in dishwasher and so on. I also see a couple of new Cadillacs in the driveway. It doesn't mean a thing."

"Really?"

"No. What counts here is credit rating. This town is full of big stars with mansions and servants and cars and mink coats. But a lot of them haven't enough cash to buy a hot dog at the beach, and they don't pay their bills."

"So you cut off their credit, naturally," I said.

"Of course. But the trouble is—" and the thought made his eyes cloud, "they just go to another store and start all over. Mr. Linkletter, you would be amazed at the big names who never pay bills, even go through bankruptcy, and can still get credit at the stores. There are always greedy merchants who will let these people charge things."

The vice president went back to his store and when he checked up on our credit rating, the furniture was promptly delivered. I never forgot that illuminating sermon. I thought at first that he was exaggerating, but I have since learned that he understated the case, if anything.

It also occurred to me, after he had gone, that he might have reached a different decision if he had looked into our so-called rumpus room.

For a while it was fashionable—and perhaps still is—for movie stars to have their own private slot machines at home. The machines helped to amuse guests who were itching to be in Las Vegas and couldn't get away, and they also paid the cost of the liquid refreshment, a substantial item on the entertainment budget in most Hollywood homes. It seemed like a sound idea to me, and with the help of some characters on whom I don't intend to blow the whistle, we got a quarter slot machine for our house.

The one-armed bandit had been whirring only a week or so when I discovered that my boy Jack, young as he was, was cadging quarters to feed the machine. Also I had to ask myself the question: *Linkletter, are you going to take money from your friends, or are you going to give them your money?* What a terrible dilemma. Obviously I couldn't clip my friends because they would soon quit coming to the house, and I was darned if I was going to give my own money away. I debated with myself for awhile, then called up a charity organization called the Goodwill Industries and told them to come after the machine. I don't know what they did with it, but I am sure it created ill will somewhere.

Perhaps I should have kept the evil machine. It might have saved me some money and solved another problem that arose when we became homeowners. I was not available for dusting, baby sitting, lawn mowing or other home chores, and Lois, who often had to go with me to dinners, parties, benefits and other personal appearances, found herself in a squeeze.

So we engaged a married couple—let's call them Mr. and Mrs. Trouble—and installed them as housekeepers.

The going rate for couples then was $350 a month, plus room and board, and the Troubles had worked for a number of movie star families. Perhaps life with the actors was less strenuous. I don't know. But they were soon quarreling as they did their work—this is one of the drawbacks in hiring a man and wife—and with every passing day they grew more careless.

There was enough debris swept under rugs to start a new dust bowl, the dishes came up with spots and the lawn looked like the haircuts on the Three Stooges. Finally, when they disappeared for two days one week without letting us know in advance, I told them to pack up their Cadillac and go.

To my pained surprise, the Troubles wrote me a note a couple of days later and said they were suing me for $22.50 in wages due. I had paid them off in full, and I was furious. Belatedly I wished I had kept the slot machine, which could easily be rigged to pay nothing at all, and they might very well have contributed $22.50 to it. Moreover, if they had asked for two hundred or even five hundred, I would have been tempted to negotiate just to avoid the unpleasant publicity that accompanies these hatchet jobs in Hollywood.

But this was one clipping I was determined to resist. I remembered what I would have done for $22.50 when I was a small boy in East San Diego, and I jumped in my car and drove to the Labor Commission office in Los Angeles. I gave my version of the dispute, and the Troubles gave theirs. The Commission threw out the case, and I never heard from the Troubles again.

I am sure this little episode will mean nothing to the scholars who will someday compile the definitive work on life in Hollywood, but it may serve as a warning to the sharpshooters that Linkletter is not a pigeon.

iv

John Guedel and I had offices in a building on the corner of Hollywood and Vine, and there I was soon learning that an entertainer's romance with the public is not as ever-loving as the fan magazines make it look.

An early disillusionment—and I certainly don't mean to discourage the practice—came when I first encountered the phenomenon of fan mail. Every major radio and television show has press agents who do everything short of smoking marijuana to get the ideas that mean publicity in every medium. Matter of fact, when I glance through my scrapbook and see some of the odd newspaper stories about me and my shows, I am not so sure that they didn't emerge from a reefer dream.

In any case, constant publicity is the lifeblood of performers and shows, and one consequence is fan mail. I do not always know what impels a man or woman in Dubuque or Miami to take the time and trouble to write to a star, but a lack of these letters is an ominous symptom that the performer is on the skids. Unfortunately, too many letters are either what we call "the bite," or they are deliberately antagonistic.

At the very beginning—when I was naïve and thin-skinned about fan mail—I got a series of venomous letters, unsigned but all in the same handwriting, from a man in San Francisco. He accused me of breaking up his home, and said he was coming to the studio to make hash out of me. We posted watchers at every entrance and had them detour any and all characters with a glazed look in their eyes. This strategy netted a number of so-called "professional contestants"—every studio has them—and they got the heave-ho. But this particular villain never showed up.

One day—I think it was on his ninth letter—the mysterious enemy absent-mindedly signed his name. Today I ignore these poison-pen missives, but at the time the letters bothered me. I was visiting in San Francisco one day, and I looked up the man's name in the phone book. He lived on one of the avenues near the beach, and on an impulse I jumped into a cab and rode to his house. The door was opened by a skinny, mousy little man and I—who am six feet two and weigh two hundred pounds—towered over him like Papa Bear did with Goldilocks.

"Art Linkletter!" he gasped.

"About those letters," I said.

He was shaking as he backed slowly into the house, and I followed. There was a small living room with a piano, and on it was a large picture of me in a silver frame. He saw me looking at it, and he exploded.

"My wife put it there," he burst out. "She talks about you all the time . . . she keeps a scrapbook about you . . . she turns you on double volume and she says why don't I do something like that . . . she makes me feel like two cents . . . and I started writing those letters to get it off my chest, but you ignored me. I was just darn sick of hearing it all the time . . . Linkletter this . . . Linkletter that."

"Take it easy," I said. "Some days *my* wife feels like that, too."

Well, we wound up kicking the ball around and shaking hands. I took the picture out of the frame and autographed it: "To John and Susie," and eventually they were both writing to me and saying that if they ever had a baby boy they would name him Art. When I get other unfriendly letters now—unfortunately there has never been an entertainer who is loved by everybody—I remember the San Francisco man, and concede that some of the opposition forces may have a legitimate peeve.

It is a statistical fact today—as it was earlier—that most of our two thousand letters a week are from people who want something.

There must be hundreds and thousands of Americans who need money for operations, rent, clothing and other things, and they are all writing to me. The prisons are filled with innocent men who could get out—or so they say—if I sent them money to hire lawyers. There are whole armies of malcontents who, if I merely mention that the sun is shining in Hollywood, deluge me with petulant remarks such as: *Who in hell cares what the weather is in Hollywood. It's colder than a snake's belly here.* There are scheming mothers who guide a child's stubby fingers so he can write me in a childish scrawl which says, in effect: *I have a club foot and I'll never be able to play in the Little League unless you send me a thousand dollars to fix it.* The variations on this Fagin-like strategy are infinite and amazing, and whenever my name is mentioned in connection with some successful business enterprise the bite mail arrives by the carload.

Not too long ago, on a steaming hot afternoon in Chichicastenango, high in the mountains of Guatemala, I saw a little girl doing bumps and grinds with a plastic hoop. There was nothing odd about that, I guess, except that they were using Spin-A-Hoops which were made by a company I own. We sold more than ten million of them—to the probable despair of parents everywhere—and I was glad to see that our salesmen had been busy in such a remote area. Anyway, one of my enterprising press agents thought my reunion with the hoops in Guatemala was worth a line or two in the papers, and I was soon drowning in a white whirlpool of letters. Lightning calculators in fifty states had estimated the company profit on ten million hoops, and they all wanted a piece of it.

It should be obvious to anyone that I cannot personally answer two thousand letters a week.

Every person who writes to me does get a reply, but I have to delegate this job to four or five girls in the office. There are days, I'm sure, when they fall behind, that they wish the postage stamp had never been invented. I am nonplused by the fact that people can sit down and send me long and deeply personal letters with their most intimate thoughts and confessions, as though I were a secret confidant—like a minister, or a family doctor. I realize that I am in their living rooms, as often as five days a week, and perhaps they consider me part of the family. It is a flattering and rewarding thought. But I am neither priest nor psychiatrist, and on such letters I have to pass.

What could I say, for instance, to the woman who wrote me this note?

> Dear Art: Perhaps some of the ladies in your audience can help solve my particular matrimonial problem.
>
> As a bride I expected a certain amount of pinching and tickling—as I remember I even enjoyed it—but at the end of a year my patience began to wear thin.
>
> To date I've acquired four children, one puppy, one kitten, three goldfish and a litter of bunnies for my husband to play with. But I still get tickled and pinched. What would you do? I've tried pinning straight pins on various parts of my anatomy in self-defense, but had to discard this practice because I'd forget they were there myself.
>
> Mrs. R. A.

If I were Dear Abby, I would have a suggestion for Mrs. R. A. that came from an early mishap on the House Party show. I was, and still am, bewitched and bewildered by the curious workings of the feminine mind, and among other things that always delighted me were women's handbags. Long ago I went into the audience one morning and impulsively opened a bag that was almost as capacious as a briefcase. Among other surprising items inside were a can opener, a canary bird pacifier, an unpaid telephone bill, a losing ticket on a horse at Bay Meadows, and a picture of Herbert Hoover. I described these coast to coast to an accompaniment of shrieking laughter, and thus a gimmick was born.

If I were a woman I would resent having my handbag explored by some clown like me.

I guess it never occurred to me that some of the charming ladies on my shows might have similar feelings, and over the years I have ruthlessly dipped into hundreds of handbags while the audience whoops and yells. I began to suspect that some of the women purposely loaded their handbags with all sorts of bizarre items on the chance that they might be singled out. In short, it was a harmless stunt and we were all having fun.

But one day I saw a woman carrying a bag that was as big and round and red as a stop sign. Perhaps I should have stopped. She looked familiar, as though she had been there often—though we openly discouraged repeaters—but I had to have a look. I picked it up, stuck my hand inside and . . . yeow! She had loaded the bag with a large rat trap, and my knuckles were bruised for days. I don't rummage around in handbags any more without first taking a cautious look inside. If this rat trap story doesn't suggest a solution to Mrs. R. A., whose anatomy gets pinched and tickled by her husband, I am afraid she will just have to relax and enjoy it.

My day is often made by the wry humor of a personal letter like the one from Mrs. R. A. But there are other notes which tell stories of heartache, and give me a pang that persists for days. A typical letter, which leaves me frustrated and floundering, is this one:

Dear Art: I would like to be on your program and win enough money to have plastic surgery on my breasts.

I am flat-chested and have tried so hard to resign myself to that fact, but this condition has made my life miserable. So many times I've said to myself: *Well, I'll just use falsies and forget it.* But when my husband reaches to caress a nonexistent breast I just die inside.

Now I have a rival. Needless to say she is *definitely* not flat-chested. But I feel that things will work out if

only I am patient and forgiving now. He has tried very
hard, but we are all prone to make mistakes.

> Unhappily yours,
> Dolores S.

Dolores is plainly the victim of what seems to be a national
neurosis in our land—an unbalanced preoccupation with the
mammary glands. Whether this is good or bad is a debate that
lies within the province of educators, social workers and
medical men. It is not something I can handle with the trite
observation that People Are Funny. What did I tell Dolores?
I said—well, it doesn't matter to anyone else. Let it be her
secret, especially since she is probably happier now.

v

One afternoon last summer when the newspapers were
printing their annual you-can-fry-eggs-on-the-sidewalk feature, I bounded out of the house and made a three-point landing
in the swimming pool. Either I had lost weight, or the elastic
in my swimming trunks was old and tired, because when I
came up—oops—my trunks had abandoned me at the bottom of
the pool and I was suddenly as naked as a peeled banana.

As I scrambled around for a towel, I heard my son Jack say
laughingly: "Well, Dad, looks as though you just answered
the weekly auction mail."

To anyone else, this may have sounded like a very cryptic
remark, but any entertainer would have understood. There has
recently been a movement—it's not a movement at all, it's a
plague—by clubs and schools and church and charity groups
everywhere to raise funds through auctions. But these are not

ordinary auctions. People are no longer selling off cakes and cookies, old books, dilapidated furniture and other familiar church bazaar items. The main items nowadays, it seems, are Frank Sinatra's shirts, Brigitte Bardot's brassière, Groucho Marx's cigars, Maria Callas' throat lozenges and so on.

It has been argued by wiser men than I that to have their elevator shoes or other personal items sold at these auctions is harmless and generates good will.

I don't quarrel with that premise, but if I sent all the clothes these organizations request—suits, shirts, shorts—I would soon be as bare as I was in the pool. I finally decided I would send nothing but neckties to these auctions, an arrangement that almost puts me out of the running.

I understand that it takes six Linkletter neckties to equal the price fetched by only one Jayne Mansfield stocking. In the teen-age set, a Ricky Nelson zipper, let's say, is worth ten Gary Cooper gun belts. Last year I donated one hundred and fifty neckties for such auctions, and I will now confess—at the risk of lowering the price to a worthless level—that I don't own that many. Through a friend of a friend I buy neckties wholesale by the hundreds—I hope this will not be a shock to the good ladies of St. Paar's Parish, the Girl Scouts or the Daughters of the American Revolution—and I send them out gladly.

I can hear the amateur auctioneers now crying out that I am thus a fake and a fraud.

Not so. Not so at all.

I put them around my neck twenty at a time, and I form them all into one big loop. Then I take them off and ship them here and there with my blessings. Please believe me when I say it—they are genuine Art Linkletter ties.

13. No Wonder I Love Women

> *A charming and witty woman I greatly admire is Ivy Baker Priest, Treasurer of the United States, whose signature appears on all our paper money.*
>
> *During one interview with her I asked: "How does it happen that pictures of women are never used on our money?"*
>
> *"Women don't care if their faces are not on the bills," she said with a smile, "as long as they can get their hands on them."*

SHAKESPEARE ONCE SAID, "Frailty, thy name is woman," and Kipling took an opposing view with his classic description, "The female of the species is more deadly than the male." Linkletter, who calls on millions of housewives every week and who is very fond of the female of the species, has never been known to coin a phrase or poetic line about women that might set off a chain reaction and leave him, inert and consumed, like a small mound of ashes at an atomic testing ground.

Actually, I stand somewhere between Shakespeare and Kipling, a cowardly attitude if there ever was one.

During my undergraduate years in Hollywood, when I was
beginning to make frequent personal appearances at banquets,
movie premieres, ball parks and drugstore openings, I had some
remarkable experiences with the ladies which proved my un-
original thesis that no man knows anything about women.
Actually, I have never really wanted to fathom the mysteries
of the female mind. I do not care to open Pandora's Box and let
the termites out.

There was the traditional little old lady, as a case in point.

I was a master of ceremonies at a show during which we
were raising money for the Community Chest, and I rashly
offered to let the highest bidder throw a chocolate meringue
pie in my face. The extent of my sacrifice can be measured by
the fact that I violently object to pie-throwing, even in slapstick comedies, and that I very nearly ended a long friendship
with comedians Olsen and Johnson because they once plastered
me with lemon pies in a Hollywood restaurant. It happened at
a private dinner party and, alas, I was not being paid for it.

Anyway, when I made my offer, a sweet little old lady
popped up in the audience and made a high bid of $250. She
was gray-haired and motherly, plus lavender and old lace. She
had an arm like Bobby Feller, and she hurled the pie with
deadly aim and a devilish laugh. Two days later, when my
ruined suit was at the cleaners, a Beverly Hills bank reported
the little old lady was a phony and had no account. I had to
pay the $250 out of my own pocket.

I was still fuming about this when I got a telephone call from
a somewhat prominent woman in Hollywood who said she had
been timing me with a stop watch.

"Timing the laughs?" I asked gaily.

"No," she snapped. "Timing your anti-Semitism."

"Oh, c'mon now," I protested, controlling my anger.

"Yes," she said. "I have figures here which show that every

time you have a guest with a Jewish name you give them from twenty-five to thirty-five seconds less than anyone else."

I told her that something would be done about her complaint, and that she would soon hear from an old friend of mine. The friend was Rabbi Edgar Magnin of Los Angeles, a noted scholar and humanitarian, and when he writes to such people about me they get a lecture I could not possibly deliver myself. I have had similar tongue lashings from Catholics, Presbyterians, Baptists, and many others—in every instance I am baffled and pained by these unjust accusations—and consequently I have formulated Linkletter's Rule No. 1: *Never talk about religion.* Rule No. 2 covers politics, and Rule No. 3, I regret to say, concerns a national decline in healthy humor.

One thought that makes me sad is that year after year, we, the American people, are inclined to laugh less and less, and especially we are unable to laugh at ourselves. Since I am talking about women here, I remember once kidding telephone operators about their various mannerisms and accents, and I was bowled over by letters saying I obviously hate telephone operators. I love telephone operators—as the switchboard girls in my exchange know—and I'm sure the telephone company loves me when they send out my big bill every month.

The old-time comedian had no problem with audiences, and could tell wonderful stories in Italian, Negro, Jewish or any other dialect without being called subversive. Today minority groups take offense at what used to be called healthy American humor, and many a big name, inadvertently using one of these dialect jokes, has had letters that would set fire to a mail box.

But I dearly love the ladies. Yes, I do.

There is Miss Lizabeth Scott, the bewitching movie star who is not exactly a member of the Linkletter fan club. She will remember, if you ask her, an evening when she appeared with me as a guest on a radio program hosted by Hildegarde. We had cooked up a little stunt in which I, wearing large diapers and a baby bib, would have Liz feeding me marshmallows as I sat on her lap. At the last moment, some executive at Paramount Pictures decided this would make their star look undignified, and I was ordered not to go through with it. Nevertheless, when the time came, I perversely decided to stick to the original idea. Liz was sitting in a chair on stage, unsuspecting, when I suddenly plopped down on her lap.

She was furious and, forgetting that the microphone was directly overhead, she snapped: "Get off me, goddammit!" The indelicate blast blistered sets from coast to coast, the sponsors recoiled, and Miss Scott hasn't spoken to me since.

I have often wondered why William Congreve, the English dramatist, wrote his immortal line about hell having no fury like a woman scorned. But now I know what he meant.

Every performer who comes into a woman's home—whether the television set is in the kitchen or the living room or the boudoir—is vulnerable to all sorts of flanking movements by women who feel that this electronic relationship is personal and intimate. Most entertainers, myself included, are aware of this potential hazard and not only employ lawyers to handle delicate situations, but also carry thousands of dollars' worth of insurance. Once in a while these precautions pay off.

Last year, during a relatively quiet moment on the House Party show, a wild-eyed woman suddenly ran on stage, spun me around as I was about to interview a small boy and cried: "Stop this show! You've ruined my life, and I won't let you do the same to this boy!"

We were on live from coast to coast, and this woman was definitely not a part of the act. The broadcast crew was so flabbergasted that none of them did anything, and for a moment I was speechless myself. A speechless Linkletter, they say, is as unlikely as a talking Sphinx, and my mind groped for an explanation. Perhaps she was a school teacher, and I had said something contrary to her beliefs. Perhaps she was the little boy's mother, and he had blurted out some family secret. I had a flash thought of one boy who, when I asked him what was the funniest sight he had seen that year, replied: "When Mom and Dad take a bath together."

But this boy had said nothing—yet. I gently asked the woman why she thought I had ruined her life.

"You just have," she said, and by this time the audience knew there was something odd about all this, "and you won't do it any more."

I was afraid she might have a gun or a knife—I don't care for either of these weapons—and so I gingerly led her into the wings and told her to go over the problem with my producer, John Guedel. The next day, because an explanation seemed in order, I told my CBS audience that we had talked to the woman. She told us I had hypnotized her as she watched me on the screen in her living room, had prevented her from coming to Hollywood to make a fortune, and thus "ruined" her life. And, just in case there were any other subjects overcome by my hypnotic personality, I looked directly into the camera, snapped my fingers commandingly as my lawyers had suggested and said: "You are hereby released from the Linkletter trance and you can all come to Hollywood to get rich."

This scene had a reasonably happy ending, but there are others which leave scars.

There was one woman, among others, who began writing me friendly little notes years ago. As the years passed, her billets-doux became affectionate, then passionate and finally downright indecent. She never signed her letters, but when she began talking about breach of promise suits and other dire penalties, my lawyers tried to track down her address. They were never able to find her though, and the letters kept coming from different cities for almost ten years.

Some months ago there came an envelope postmarked London, England, and I recognized the now familiar writing. I opened it, and pulled out a note on scented paper, and a small snapshot.

> "I can at last tell you my name," she said. "I have found a husband here, and I have finally gotten you out of my system. I am sending the photo of myself because I want you to know that I am still beautiful and desirable. You could have had me if you had only once mentioned me on your programs. I would have come to you.
>
> Jane S."

I looked at the picture and I was sorry that I had been so aggravated by her notes. Her face was pinched and bony, and there was a deep scar across one cheek. The thin mouth was unsmiling, and there was a mortal hurt in the large round eyes. I turned the picture over and in another handwriting was this message:

> "Dear Mr. Linkletter: I am Jane's sister, and I just want to say she will never bother you again. She wrote this letter in the hospital where she died last week.
>
> "P. S. She told you one little lie but perhaps you will understand. She had no husband at all."

ii

For me to repeat that there's nothing like a dame, either here or in the South Pacific, is a redundance for which I hope to be forgiven.

With the House Party show going into millions of homes

every day at an hour when the man of the house is slaving away
at the office, it seems normal and natural that I should be interested in women and my small contribution to their daily lives.
On the other hand, their contributions to my life have been
immeasurable, a harvest few men can equal.

Over the years Lois and I have counted hundreds of gifts
from these faithful friends. We have had giant watermelons
from Texas, mammoth potatoes from Idaho. There is one
woman who regularly sends Scandinavian pastries, another who
shipped a barrel of lobsters from Maine. As our children were
born, they were outfitted with booties and blankets and diapers
by the carload, and we have received enough cookies, cakes,
rolls and pies to stock a bakery. We have sampled these goodies
for years and will go right on nibbling despite the admonition
of one macabre friend who said: "I wouldn't touch the stuff
with *your* shows. The next cake may be iced with cyanide."

We think with sweet remembrance of a Berkeley widow
named June Nahl, who knitted argyle socks for me once a year
and sent cleverly woven sweaters to our kids. When she was
stricken with an incurable disease a year or two back, she
wasted away in a matter of weeks, and on the day of her death
wrote me this note as a nurse steadied her hand: "Dear Art and
Lois: I am going now. I am not afraid to die because I had the
joy in life of knowing you two, and your fine children. My
only regret is that I cannot stay to watch them grow."

To go from the sublime to the ridiculous, Lois and I have
been given enough turtles to make endless turtle neck sweaters.
In our freezer there is a box of frozen whale blubber sent to
me by some Eskimo friends. I have had a dahlia named after
me, and somewhere around the house is a shrunken human
head which, despite the donor's insistence, is not all that remains
of Mr. Terry O'Flaherty, the television critic for the San
Francisco *Chronicle* who persists in voting me "Abominable

Showman No. 1." Up in our attic is a bale of llama wool—a gift from a woman in South America—that might be useful when llama wool makes a comeback. We call it llama's bank account. I own a live baby elephant which was shipped to me by friends in India, and I have loaned it to the Los Angeles Zoo. A Texas woman mailed me a live bull—imagine the postage due on that!—and I gave it to Gene Autry, who has a number of brown cows.

I also have a mental gallery of some other women who enriched what might otherwise have been dull days.

There was the gentle little woman on my show whom I asked: "What was the outstanding quality about your son when he was a small boy?"

"He was the greatest potato peeler in the family," she said.

The mother was Hannah Nixon, and her potato-peeling son is Richard M. Nixon.

There was the late Miss Jean Harlow, the breathtaking siren of the Thirties who, when I was all of seventeen and made a tentative pass, looked at me sweetly and said: "You're a nice little boy. But isn't your mother worried about your being up so late?"

Among the hundreds of autograph collectors—they are hiding behind every bush and telephone pole no matter where I go—there was a woman who chopped me down to size. Lois and I were driving into Beverly Hills for one of those plush movie openings, and with us were Edgar Bergen and his pretty wife, Frances. As I slowed the car in front of the theater, we were engulfed by a swarm of autograph collectors, and I heard a shrill voice crying: "Hey, there's Edgar Bergen!"

Bergen expertly and happily signed half a dozen pads, then one of the signature chasers stuck her head through the open front window, looked at me and said: "Hey, are you anybody?"

"No," I said. "I'm Mr. Bergen's chauffeur."

Bergen snickered and accused me of using a quip that was old when Charlie McCarthy still had sap running through him. But I went into the theater, hardly bleeding at all, and mumbling to myself about the ephemeral nature of fame. I was thinking that even a nobody is a somebody and, had I been as lethal with the sharp ad lib as my press agents claim, I might have squelched her. I should have said: *My name is Art Linkletter and I'll be glad to get your television set repaired.* Or, perhaps, I simply should have said my name was Linkletter and let her figure out the mystery herself.

iii

There is one woman whose gentle face is always before me, whose voice I hear when there is silence in the house, and whose gnarled hands still seem to be shyly touching my shoulders when my thoughts are blue.

Mary Linkletter was the only mother I ever had, and yet I know, had we ever talked about it, she would have said: "Artie . . . I could never seem to give you what I wanted to give." But she gave more than she ever knew, for she was selfless, fiercely loyal and never bitter about her quarantined life. It was an empty life in many ways—empty in the sense that she was my father's shadow, serving him dawn to dusk, dedicated to his needs, patient in the drab routine of their narrow little world.

I had always thought of her looking out on life through a small window, never seeing the wide sweep of sky and the hills and valleys beyond, never quite feeling the beating pulse of people. I wanted her to know the sights and sounds and sensations that had been denied her all those long years, and when Father Linkletter died I tried again to move her to a home of her own. Near us, perhaps, where she could see the grandchildren she loved, where she would not have to limit herself to two or three visits a year as she was doing.

But she chose to stay in the Pomona apartment, and there she insisted on the Spartan routine she had always known. She climbed ladders to fix drapes or lights, she cooked her own meals and made the bed and knitted and sewed, and took her lonely walks along the street.

In the entertainment business there seems to be automatic license for the public to pry into the closed pages of a performer's daily life.

The stars may not like it, they may grumble and protest that personal privacy is a privilege and a right, but at the same time they not only permit people to peer into their windows, but in many cases they urge their press agents to open closed doors. Consequently those in the secondary ranks—the children, parents and even servants of a star—are caught up in this light and are included in the scene. I know many a star whose parents or other relatives share the publicity and, understandably, do it with pride.

But not Mother Linkletter.

It is a curious fact, I think, that in all the hundreds and thousands of stories that have been printed about me and my family, there has been very little said about Mary Linkletter. She wanted anonymity, and she got it. We were never photographed together. When she came to one of my shows—and that was a rare event—she sat in the most distant row and never, as most mothers would have done, turned to a woman alongside and said: "That's my boy Artie. I'm his mother."

She was eighty-six years old when I finally persuaded her that the television set I had given her was not an instrument of evil, and at last, reluctantly, she let the light flicker from the tube into her little living room. She had never seen a motion picture in a theater, nor had she ever knowingly permitted me inside a movie house. Now, near the end of life, she was seeing the wonders of a once forbidden world. I was secretly amused —though I never let her know—to learn that she, like millions of other women, was watching the late, late show, and that she was fascinated by the grunts and grimaces of the wrestlers, faking triumph or defeat on the television screen.

Then one night she suddenly slipped back in her big chair, and her eyes saw nothing but the bare walls, and she was dying a little and did not know.

She could no longer cook her simple meals, nor dress herself, nor take the walks, and I knew that she had lived her life. We prayed that she would be taken gently, without pain and without ever realizing that she could never be left alone again. I put her into a sanitarium where she could have care, but the sun was going down and she left us on a gray January morning in 1957.

She had wanted the Twenty-third Psalm read at her funeral, and it was. I think it spoke more for her than any words my father had ever said. "Surely goodness and mercy shall follow me all the days of my life, and I will dwell in the House of the Lord forever."

I am sure she will.

14. State Trouper

Some years ago I was invited to be master of ceremonies at the world premiere of pianist Liberace's first movie. Liberace was standing beside me outside the theater as the celebrities arrived, and he was dazzling in an overcoat of white sheared beaver.

Most Hollywood stars have no imagination and the best they can do in a brief moment is to say: "So happy to be here tonight. I'm sure the picture will be great." There had been a few of these uninspired nothings, and then William Bendix came up to the microphone and took one incredulous look at Liberace's coat.

"Bill Bendix!" I exclaimed. "What do you have to say?"

"Well . . ." he replied. "I have only one word of advice for Liberace: Don't eat anything with gravy on it."

Two years ago a farm magazine in Des Moines, Iowa, made a survey to determine whether certain nationally known personalities could be easily recognized or identified by Midwestern farmers.

The results of the poll showed that more than ninety per cent of the farmers instantly recognized me, but only fifty per cent could identify Senator William Knowland of California or Senator John Kennedy of Massachusetts. I don't know why the magazine bracketed me with these distinguished gentlemen (unless there was some subtle political water-witching involved), but it was flattering to me, and you can be sure my sponsors were impressed.

The real reason so many people know me, of course, is that old device known as the personal appearance, or what we in the trade call exposure—with or without a white sheared beaver coat.

I am certain that none of the farmers who were polled had stopped plowing or harvesting long enough to catch my afternoon television show. It is much more probable that they had seen me on a Saturday or Sunday in the fair grounds, an armory, a ball park or a high school auditorium. During the period when I was clawing and scratching to get my shows into the top ten, I covered more miles around the country than all the thousands of traveling salesmen who ever pursued a farmer's daughter.

I had long been convinced that the personal appearance was an absolute must. Like the man at the shotgun wedding who had a choice of wife or death, I felt that either I could stay in Hollywood and remain an inaccessible image and perhaps fade out in time, or I could hit the road and meet the people.

There are not too many entertainers in Hollywood who understand the challenge of the personal appearance. In the studio, with an intimate audience of perhaps three hundred, and with technicians and assistants rigidly controlling every facet of the show, almost nothing ever gets out of hand. But when you play a race track in Sioux Falls, South Dakota, with the temperature at 105 and little eddies of dust blinding your eyes, and face a sweltering and irritable audience—as I did once —then you have been melted down to size.

I was surprised and dismayed, on these journeys of mine, to

find that a seasoned performer, supposedly familiar with every
kind of crisis, could occasionally be as helpless as a canary out
of a cage. The customer in a distant city, who has paid from
three to six dollars for a seat, bears no resemblance to the one
in the Hollywood studio audience who gets in with a free
ticket.

There are several other hazards on these road trips and there
is no guaranteed protection against them.

For instance, when you are in a downtown hotel room in
Chicago or Boston or anywhere else, you are as naked as a
plucked chicken. There are no studio guards to keep out the
screwballs, no roped lines to hold back the crowd, no assistants
to lie and say you've just left for Hong Kong.

I know a number of celebrities who won't make personal
appearances because they are afraid of the inevitable swarm of
amateur photographers. They don't want to be caught with
their hair out of place or their wrinkles showing, but I have
never backed away from a camera lens. I happily urge people
to shoot up a whole roll, because it so happens that I'm a large
stockholder in Eastman Kodak. And besides, I have no wrinkles.
Well . . . only a few.

Personal appearances also leave you wide open for hecklers.

The word heckle is a variant of hatchel, an instrument used
for cutting up flax or hemp, and it fits. When I was first learning how to be a master of ceremonies, I was angered and
thrown off balance by hecklers, and I wished I had the flint-
tipped quips Joe E. Lewis always had ready. I remembered
hearing him say to one loud pest: "Sir, the last time I saw a
mouth like yours it had a hook in it."

But in time I developed a skin like an armadillo, and I found
that in certain situations I could fire back without using cracks
from old joke books. I was in Cincinnati once, doing a show
with a large audience, and I selected a man in a back row to ask

the key question of the program: "What is tall, white and dependable?" I was standing beside my sponsor's product, a large home refrigerator, and the man was supposed to mention it by name so I could follow up with the commercial.

Instead—and there is always one such wise guy in every audience—he decided to get into the act himself. "You must mean my wife," he said.

With my regular commercial ruined, I located this character's wife in the audience and asked her to stand up. "I can see she's tall and certainly white," I said. "But does she have a built-in quick-freeze?"

Suddenly confused, the man answered: "Yes."

"And—" I went on, "does her upper compartment have room for seventy pounds of food?"

At this point the audience was convulsed, and the amateur comedian was dragged out by his smoldering wife. I know just how they felt. I once made the mistake of trying to trade quips with Milton Berle at a banquet, and when his turn came he said: "Yes, sir, Art. People are funny. But in your case forget it."

ii

If my grandchildren gather around me some long winter night twenty years from now and ask me to talk about my travels, I can dig up a memory or two.

I think one of the worst personal appearance shows I ever lived through was in a ball park in Terre Haute, Indiana. It was a cold blustery night, and there weren't enough people there to start a good crap game. I was throwing my gags from the pitcher's mound, and they all went foul before they ever got to the audience, huddled in blankets and cussing themselves for paying $3.50 to catch pneumonia.

And I can recall a show in a Colorado mining town, a booking I had accepted only because there was a lead mine in the neighborhood that had investment possibilities. Well, they never got the lead out, either in the theater or out of the mine.

I remember playing the State Fair in Syracuse, when prize cattle were dropping dead from the heat. So were my stunts and gags.

I think of an evening performing in the vastness of Soldier's Field in Chicago, where the echo throws back the jokes two days later, by which time they have been stolen by ten other comedians and used on competing shows.

I can still see a dead-pan audience in a certain town in Oklahoma, where I had gone to do a show because some trusted adviser touted me on an oil field there. I not only laid an egg, but I left five thousand dollars behind to start drilling a well. Sometime afterward, one of my puckish partners sent me this telegram:

> Struck ketchup at six thousand feet. Drilled into hamburger stand abandoned during dust storm in early Thirties. Estimate we need five thousand more to locate mustard.

I sent the extra five but that vanished, too. I can't bear to look at hamburgers any more.

I shudder when I think of one town in the deep South where the lighting in the theater was so poor I couldn't see the people in the distant rows, and where I was staging a dancing contest with a man and woman chosen at random from the audience. When my ushers brought the couple to the stage to start dancing, the woman was one of the town's white social leaders, and the man turned out to be a Negro preacher. I had to abandon the dance contest on the spot, and awarded them the prize without further ado. I don't know what the orchestra was playing, but it should have been the popular tune that goes: "Did you ever see a bad dream walking? Well, I did."

For all of these embarrassing incidents, though, there were others that balanced the books. There was one in particular—it was somewhere in Ohio, I think—that came up with an ending which left me, for one of the few times in my life, totally speechless. One of our contest prizes that evening was an expensive mink stole, and I draped it around the shoulder of the winner, a plain little woman who blushed and stammered her thanks.

"Wait until your husband sees you in this," I said. "I bet he'll say you're beautiful."

"He's here in the audience," she said.

"Great," I said. "Let's bring him up for a close look."

Our ushers located the man and led him up to the stage and I suddenly realized with a sinking heart that he was completely blind. I was tongue-tied and my mind fumbled for some out. But I need not have worried, because here was a man who needed no help from me. "You're absolutely right, Mr. Linkletter," he said. "I can see that she is beautiful."

iii

I've never had any regrets about the thousands of miles I have traveled for personal appearances (and continue to travel), nor about the flops and troubles and disappointments I may have had on the road.

I have seen the face and heart of America.

The television camera that photographs me every day is no longer a mere mechanical eye, with its little red warning light. To me it is a window looking into millions of homes, and I like to feel that in each of them I am one of the family. I can see Canal Street in New Orleans, and Biscayne Bay in Miami, and the quiet waters of Puget Sound in Seattle, and a thousand other places because I have been there. I can even see the batter's box in the ball park at Cleveland, because a skeptical sports writer, hearing that I was supposed to be a fair athlete, once planted me there with a bat in my hand. The pitcher was the great Mel Harder, and the sports writer said: "It's a hundred to one you never even see the ball." I smacked the first pitch over second base for what would have been a double, and from that day to this I have wisely never swung a bat again.

There are some drawbacks to these expeditions, of course, which I have vainly tried to overcome.

In many cities there are men and women who will tell their friends in great confidence that they are responsible for my success. I have heard of at least three who claim they dreamed up the format for People Are Funny, and there are just as many who take credit for the House Party idea. These unsung collaborators don't trouble me at all. They are walking billboards for me, and are not likely to spread anti-Linkletter sentiments around. But there is a group of self-appointed critics at large in many cities who are convinced that I am suffering from a bad case of the swollen head. It is these people who exasperate me because no explanation seems to do much good.

During the past twenty-five years—with more than a hundred and fifty thousand broadcasts behind me—I have met thousands of people, from the President of the United States down to the lowliest bootblack on a side street in Memphis. I simply cannot remember them all. I often wish I had the memory credited to former Postmaster Jim Farley, who not only knew the names of thousands of voters but could chat familiarly about their neighborhood, their kids and their dogs.

I often go to an affair out of town where I am greeted by some man, and the dialogue goes like this:

"Hello, Art. Long time no see."

"Hi—everything okay?"

"Look—" he says, "you don't remember me, do you?"

"Let's see—" I reply, fumbling, "it was at—"

"Yeah, I thought you didn't remember. It was at that big press party."

Press party? I've been to hundreds. Why doesn't this idiot be specific? Why doesn't he tell me his name? I am beginning to burn a little. So is he.

"Oh, well," he says, and now he has the stinger out, "I guess you meet people more important than me. Anyhow, I knew you when."

And he walks away, as sour as curdled milk, and from then on he tells people what a stinker I am.

Another problem that often gums up an otherwise happy personal appearance tour is the autograph collector. I do not understand the compulsion that makes people collect autographs, stamps, matchbooks, beer bottle caps or blondes—well, the blondes I can understand—but I do agree with everyone else in Hollywood that when the collectors stop asking for your signature you are ready for the ash can.

I am pleased and flattered, indeed, when people ask for my autograph, but I have the plaintive wish that they wouldn't do it just when I am beginning to sample the soup in a restaurant, or when I am obviously engaged in an important conversation with some friend. I would like to see all autograph collectors organize an association and have a code of ethics which, among other rules, would make it a misdemeanor to ask for a signature when the performer is flat on his posterior. I was at the Winter Olympic Games in Squaw Valley last year, valiantly learning to ski—a grievous error at my age—when one of those confounded wooden slats flipped me over. I slid down fifty feet of ice and snow, and I was lying there, bruised and vanquished, with snow masking my face, when three young women knelt down beside me. I thought they were ministering angels from the Ski Patrol, but they cried out in unison: "Mr. Linkletter—please give us your autograph." They had neither book nor pencil, and frankly I was simmering.

"I'm not Linkletter," I said. "That's him standing over there by the ice rink."

I pointed to a tall young man surrounded by a group of Olympic officials, and they went running. I wish I could have seen their faces when they pounced on this innocent young fellow and saw that he was not Art Linkletter at all but a visitor named Richard M. Nixon.

There are collectors, incidentally—as every celebrity knows —who get in line when you are rapidly signing your name to match covers, menus and assorted scraps of paper and who use that hoary trick of slipping you a blank check. Some of my friends in show business resent this gimmick and angrily tear up the checks, but I have a strategy of my own. When some joker hands me a check, I fill it out so that it reads: "Pay to the order of Art Linkletter—$10,000."

Needless to say, none of these little frictions—and in the great beauty and spread of my personal horizon they are microscopic—will stop me from traveling to the far places of America and the world. Every state and town and village has new sights and sounds and people, and each mile of the most distant journey is a rebirth for me. I am the original Cook's Tour man, and I get my reward in the discoveries that are never mentioned in the tourist guides. Just to set down a fragment that comes to mind, I was in Istanbul a year or two ago, and I sent this cable to Hedda Hopper in Hollywood:

> Have had many a turkey on radio and television, but this is the first time have ever been inside one. What a place for bargains! Am bringing you back an old used sultan.
>
> Love—Art Linkletter

I was still in Istanbul, enjoying the stuffing, when Hedda cabled back:

> Make it a young one.
>
> Love—Hedda.

You know—I might find her one at that.

15. The Last Angry Man

There was a boy on the House Party show one morning and he was talking about his father who was advertising manager for a mattress company.

"Just what does your dad do?" I asked.

"He writes the slogans for the ads," he replied.

"For instance?"

"Well," the boy said, "the one they use now says: 'Sleeping on our mattress is like sleeping on a cloud.'"

"That's very clever," I said, "and thanks for telling us."

"Yeah," the boy went on, "but at home we say it's like sleeping on a clod."

THERE IS AN old Linkletter axiom which says: "Only *children* tell the truth."

I may have to amend that momentarily because there are some truths I wish to discuss here, including the fact that the glamorous life in Hollywood too often is like sleeping on a clod, to use my young friend's phrase.

When my two television programs became fixtures—a fixture in my business is any show that doesn't fold after a season or two—I found that my name was getting on the charity bite-list more and more. And I have now reached a point where I have to say what most Hollywood stars know but won't admit out loud: *Charity organizations are making liars of us all.*

In the fund-raising field it is a recognized fact that celebrities mean money in the bank. It is not news to say that entertainers are among the few people in the world who continually give away the only commodity they have to sell. Most performers are notoriously soft touches when that over-worked word, "charity," is involved, and there are promoters in Hollywood who sit up half the night dreaming up new schemes to trick the stars into working for nothing.

This aggravates me, frankly, and I think it's time to expose it.

The system has two or three tested strategies. In the first, you get a phone call from a committeeman representing an established and worthwhile charity. He wants you to headline a fund-raising show and he gives you a certain date. You protest that you have an incredibly crowded schedule—which is true—that you are exhausted or need a vacation or would like to spend some time with your family.

"Ah, but this is *very special*, Art," he says.

You repeat your tale of woe and regretfully decline. An hour later you get a phone call from an important network executive or a big name producer. "Art," he says ominously, "this shindig happens to be your sponsor's pet charity, if you know what I mean." I know what he means. I don't have to be hit by a truck to get the point. So I go. After four or five of these pitches I do what other performers do. I become a liar. I tell them that I am going to be in New York or London or almost anywhere.

I have appeared at hundreds of benefits and charity affairs and I will continue doing it, especially for those organizations to whom I owe so much—such as the YMCA—but I resent being swindled or blackmailed.

Device No. 2, for instance, is ingeniously deadly and there

is almost no counterattack to beat it. In this maneuver the committee chairman—usually a woman with the gushy bird-brain mannerisms made famous by Billie Burke—says: "Oh . . . Mr. Linkletter . . . the most awful thing has happened. We're in a terrible fix about our charity dinner . . . someone was supposed to call you . . . she assumed another woman already had . . . and everybody just took for granted you had accepted."

"But I haven't accepted," I say.

Then comes the *coup de grâce.* "Oh, how miserable! You see . . . the programs are all printed . . . the tickets with your name on them are all sold out . . . the publicity has gone out . . . why, right this minute your picture is already in the paper. We're *so* sorry."

As of that moment they've got you. And if you don't show up you're a creep and a no-good to all those who bought tickets.

The third gimmick is so insidious as to assume the proportions of a racket.

Let's say that the Cirrhosis Anonymous Association is running short of both publicity and money, so they hold an emergency meeting with their press agent. If he knows his business he comes up with a brilliant idea, saying: "We will proclaim Art Linkletter the best television personality of 1960 and we will give him a handsome plaque, suitably engraved. We will present him with the plaque on his House Party show, and thus millions of people will hear about Cirrhosis Anonymous."

They order the plaque, they call me with the exciting news and they want to know when they can appear on the show. When I say no, the plaque is thrown into the nearest garbage can, and suddenly I am no longer the best television personality of 1960.

During the past ten years, I have been singled out for overwhelming honors—handsomest nose, shiniest shoes, happiest smile, cleanest comedian, and so on. But I was coldly stripped of these awards, like a soldier traitor who has the buttons cut from his uniform, when in each instance it turned out that I could not or would not attend the presentation ceremonies in person. To say nothing of entertaining the audience for an hour or so.

Somewhere in Hollywood, hidden away like a Tennessee mountain still, there must be a little factory secretly manufacturing plaques, medals, cups and other awards for hundreds of press agents who have discovered that this is a painless and inexpensive way to get their clients a plug. I am not exaggerating when I say that I am offered an average of three hundred plaques or scrolls a year, but I never actually get them unless I attend the banquet ceremonies or accept them on a television show. I have since made an inflexible rule that I will not accept any such honors—and a good many of these offers are legitimate—if the presentation has to be made on my television shows.

It is a cold, ruthless business, as you can see.

I do not intend this to be a sermon against the recognized charities which do such wonderful work—the Cancer Fund, the Red Cross, the Heart Fund, and many others. But I do fight the phonies and the slick operators and the unctuous promoters who call you only because you can deliver money or talent. The only wry humor in this situation is a remark once made by George Gobel. "Walter Winchell has been a blessing to the Cancer Drive," he said. "Bob Hope is tied up with the Cerebral Palsy Fund, and Eddie Cantor has done great work for the Heart campaign. By the time they got around to me, all the good diseases were taken."

One morning last year, I had a telephone call from a very

prominent and influential woman in Hollywood. She was an executive associate of a motion picture potentate whose name you would instantly recognize, and she was chairman of a committee for a major benefit.

She talked to me for ten minutes, telling me how much I had contributed to radio and television, how much all of Hollywood loved me and my wife and children, and how vital it was for me to attend the affair.

"Art," she said, "I just can't tell you what it would mean to have you handling the show for us."

I looked at my calendar and said: "I'm terribly sorry, but I'll be out of town on a personal appearance tour all that week."

"Oh . . ." she said. There was a dull click, and I jiggled the hook. "Hello . . . hello!" I said.

I hung up, thinking we had been disconnected, and waited. Ten minutes went by, and the phone was silent. I suddenly realized that she had deliberately hung up on me because I did not agree to the date. I was infuriated, particularly since I actually did have an out-of-town date, and I never spoke to her again. I avoid her at Hollywood parties, and I will never again participate in any of her benefits.

There are, of course, some banquets and dinners and benefits that I never turn down. Nor does anyone else.

These are the testimonial affairs given by the Friars and the Masquers Clubs, honoring some star for his or her contribution to show business, and they are command performances.

The guests in each instance are the highest paid artists, directors, writers and producers in the world. The material, which is strictly inside stuff or shop talk, is risqué, hilarious and new. When Bob Hope or Jack Benny or Danny Thomas is assigned to emcee one of these star-studded banquets, you can be sure their writers will lose sleep for many a night, creating off-the-record gags and comedy routines that will have their brief moment of life and never be heard again.

The moral in all this, as many a Hollywood star has realized with a heavy heart, is that when you are no longer useful you are as good as embalmed.

We are in an ephemeral business. The star blazes high across the sky and then it burns out. The drop is rapid, painful and final. I know very well that one day—when I am no longer on the air—I will quickly join the forgotten men. And this is one of the reasons I am savoring every minute of my day, looking around at all the other good things in the world, and staying actively involved in business and industry. No man will ever be able to point me out on the street and say: "Look—there goes poor old Art Linkletter. Used to be a big star. Big money. But he blew it."

ii

There was a time when, like any other amateur in the presence of champions, I was squirming like the small boy on his first visit to dancing school. I had the firm conviction that the old pros looked down their noses at my offbeat style. Radio masters of ceremonies represented a new and almost undefinable art form that was not learned in years of struggling with audiences on beat-up vaudeville stages. I felt that they thought of me as an upstart, a Johnny-come-lately who didn't belong on the same boards with the men and women who were born in a backstage trunk, so to speak, and who suffered long years to polish and perfect their technique.

But it was not that I wanted to be a comedian like the others.

It was only that I wanted to be accepted on equal terms with my special brand of entertainment. I finally made it, but there were some crash landings along the way. I liked to think that in certain situations my mind automatically applied a humorous twist. I thought I could go almost anywhere and come up with some funny ad libs about the most trifling incident, and I depended on that ability to get by.

Lois knew I leaned on my glibness, and one day she looked at me gravely and asked: "Art—what's going to happen if you suddenly run into a dead end on this stuff?"

"Then I'll quit," I said.

Another time we were driving along Sunset Boulevard, en route to an important dinner and Lois casually asked: "What are you going to talk about tonight?"

"I don't know, honey," I said. "It'll come out when I get there."

So there came an evening when I was invited to speak at the Annual Parade of Champions at the Biltmore Hotel in Los Angeles. This dinner is sponsored by the Los Angeles *Times*, with sport champions flown in from every corner of the land, and I was on the dais as the principal speaker. I had not written anything in advance, and while we were dining—as was my custom—I furiously scribbled down all sorts of quips and funny observations about the athletes there.

By the time we got through the dessert, I had a formidable list of humorous remarks, and I was ready to start when Braven Dyer, sports editor of the *Times*, and chairman of the program stood up.

"Ladies and gentlemen," he said, "before we start I want to take a moment to introduce an old friend who just happened to drop in tonight. He is not on the program but I want him to stand up and take a bow."

The unexpected guest turned out to be Bob Hope. He not

only took a bow . . . maybe three or four bows, in fact . . .
but he began to talk. He went on for ten minutes, using
situations similar to the ones I had so carefully jotted down
for my own use, and he had that banquet screaming. I was
desperately hoping there would be a bomb scare or an explosion in the boiler room, or any disaster that would put an end
to my agony and clear the hall. I was left sitting there like an
empty gas tank, and I never forgot it.

Hope didn't murder me deliberately, of course. He might
not have been introduced. He wasn't on the program. But he
had been ready—just in case. As all comedians are ready, any
time, anywhere. The old master taught me a lesson that night,
and I'm grateful for it. When I go out tomorrow night or
next week or next year, I'll be ready. It might be a dinner for
tomato stuffers or belt stretchers or bilge pumpers, but I'll be
ready. No one but Lois knows—and this is the first time I have
said it publicly—that I have gone to literally hundreds of
dinners, meetings and socials where I have neither been introduced nor asked to say a few words. But in my pocket each
time was a sheaf of notes and jokes and anecdotes. Did I say
I was an ad-lib man? I take it all back.

iii

The show must go on—they say—and so must Linkletter.
I have been asked over and over again to be toastmaster for
the Friars and Masquers testimonial dinners, and during the
past ten years there has been only one tragedy. The story has
not been told before, and I am revealing it here only because
it reminds me of one of Father Linkletter's favorite quotations
from the Book of John—one that means so much to me as I

grow older: "Walk while ye have the light, lest darkness come upon you."

The Friars banquet on this occasion was held November 23, 1958. It was a charity dinner for the City of Hope Hospital and the Friars were presenting their cherished award to two fine people in show business—Lucille Ball and Desi Arnaz. It was a singular privilege for me to be the master of ceremonies of a program with the entertainment provided by George Murphy, Tony Martin, Milton Berle, Dean Martin, George Burns, Danny Thomas, Sammy Davis, Jr., and Harry "Parkyakarkus" Einstein.

The dinner was a white-tie affair in the International Ballroom of the Beverly-Hilton Hotel.

Every major star in Hollywood was there, and there were enough diamonds in sight to dim the lights of Broadway. It was a happy, noisy, laughing and memorable evening, and the entertaining stars were never better for an audience that could be described as the most critical and discerning of all. George Burns had just completed one of his great routines—in Hollywood he is known as the comedian's comedian—and I was about to introduce Harry Einstein, whose garbled Greek as Parkyakarkus had regaled Eddie Cantor's radio audiences for years. Lucille Ball, sitting next to me, gave me a nudge.

"Look at Harry," she whispered. "I'd give anything to be as calm and assured as he is."

"Don't let him fool you," I said softly. "I know him. He's dying inside. He hasn't eaten all day and his insides are crawling with tension. That poise he puts on is a great act."

A moment later I presented Einstein to the crowd, and he delivered a monologue about the Friar's Club that had his listeners weeping with laughter. I recall that he said the club had the largest pool in the West, but you couldn't swim in it because it was a football pool. He mentioned the club's beautiful new library and said that someday they hoped to get a book. "We also have a nature study group in the club," he said. "They are especially interested in bird-watching. Any day you'll see two or three members standing around the game room looking for a pigeon."

These lines may not have the same impact in print as they had with his drawling delivery and his wonderful sense of timing, but I have never heard a more thunderous sound when he sat down, wiping the glistening beads from his forehead.

"I have heard Harry entertain many times," I commented to the audience, "and each time I've asked myself: Why doesn't he have a program of his own on prime time on a major television network."

Harry smiled and nodded his thanks and suddenly there was a frightening emptiness in his eyes, as though a shade had been drawn to shut out the light. His head dropped forward, and as he sprawled there, Ed Wynn rushed up from a nearby table and cried: "Art! He's having a heart attack! Get some nitroglycerin tablets."

I grabbed the microphone, banged the gavel and called out: "Has anyone got any nitroglycerin? Please bring it here in a hurry."

There was a stampede of feet, and to my astonishment I saw many famous stars and powerful producers thrusting their hands at me, and in each there was a small vial of nitroglycerin tablets. We stuffed them frantically into Harry's mouth, and lifted him gently and carried him backstage. The room was deathly still, and I motioned to Danny Thomas, who was next on the program. He knew what I was thinking. The show must go on. But he shook his head violently, and now someone came out from behind the curtain and made a curious little motion with his thumb. And so we knew Harry Einstein, in his hour of triumph, had gone away and would never be back.

I stood there with a sinking heart, and I'm afraid that for a moment I had some bitter thoughts. I looked on either side of the head table, and at the tablets just below the dais, and remembered what a ruthless scramble there had been for these choice seats, and that some of these people had even offered bribes to make sure that their table was in the status group.

Now Harry Einstein was dead, and they all wanted out.

And I could only say: "Ladies and gentlemen, we have all been hurt by a terrible tragedy here, and I know the evening is over. I want to take just one moment to do what we came here for—to present our medal to Desi Arnaz."

So Desi walked up to me, and he saw that I had the medal in my hand. And I was thinking of this puny piece of metal and how small and useless it was at that moment. And Desi stared at it with brimming eyes and took it and said: "A few minutes ago this medal was the most important thing in the world. Now it doesn't mean a damn thing."

He stuck it in his pocket and walked away.

There are rare moments, even in Hollywood, when the truth is blurted out.

iv

In the public mind—and I am probably as culpable as my press agents—I am thought of as a friendly man whose head is not cluttered up with unhappy thoughts.

The critics and other newspaper writers have given me all sorts of saccharine labels—toothy, grinning, genial, wholesome, debonair—ad nauseam. I naturally wonder if my son Jack had these adjectives in mind a few summers ago when we were traveling in France, and he disagreed with me on some decision I had made. In fact, he got so hot-headed about it that he took a punch at me. I put a judo hold on him and threw him across the room so hard that his head rattled. "If you get up off the floor," I said, "I'll knock your teeth out."

Jack was not the first boy who decided he could lick his dad, but he missed, and he sat on the floor looking at me, not angrily, but incredulously.

"Why, Dad," he said. "I didn't know you could get mad."

Jack is a lot huskier these days, and I have laughingly told him I would be in a cast for a week if I tried wrestling with him now. But he will understand why I am relating this incident for the first time. I am not always genial, wholesome, grinning and happy. Like most of us, I have a fair assortment of pet peeves in addition to the charity subject I have just discussed, and I want to talk about them.

One day last spring the four little children on my House Party program were with our regular teacher, Mrs. Dorothy Gillespie, on their guided tour of the CBS studios. This tour is an educational trip for the youngsters and is a daily ritual, and on that morning they wandered into an unoccupied set of the Playhouse 90 show, which was directed by a young and brilliant man named John Frankenheimer.

Frankenheimer was there, and in no uncertain terms he told them to beat it. Four weeks later, the teacher and another group of children unfortunately strolled across one of Frankenheimer's empty stages during a rehearsal break while he was in a control booth above them. He turned on the loudspeaker system and bellowed: "Get those brats out of here!"

The kids retreated in frightened confusion, and were still jumpy when they took their places on my show. As we went on the air, I asked one small boy what he liked best about the trip to the studio.

"Well," he said, "I liked the ride in the big limousine but Mr. Linkletter, I sure don't like that Frankenstein down there."

That did it for me, and for the first time in my television life I blew up on camera. "That *is* the right name for that fellow you're talking about," I said. "His real name is Frankenheimer and he's the director of one of our biggest shows. But his name should be Frankenstein, because he is an arrogant young pup who is throwing his weight around, as he did with you kids, and he has earned the dislike of almost everyone in this building."

We were on live in Eastern states for this show, with a taped repeat scheduled for the West Coast that afternoon. I suspect that my blast rattled windows all over the building and in two seconds flat Frankenheimer had a verbatim report. He rushed upstairs to the executive offices and demanded that my remarks be deleted for the West Coast showing. The bosses refused, and Frankenheimer then yelled for his lawyers but there was nothing they could do.

At two-thirty, when my show was repeated, he heard my cracks all over again and promptly issued a series of statements that cut me up in small pieces.

I have had no further contact with Frankenheimer since then, but there were some strange aftermaths. Innumerable stars, directors and technicians called or came by my office to thank me for taking on a man who, because of his talent and explosive temperament, had previously been handled with kid gloves. One nationally syndicated columnist phoned and said: "Art—what do you want me to print about this character?"

"Nothing," I said. "Let's forget it. I don't want to be involved in a silly running feud."

Presently I noticed that the Playhouse 90 stage was plastered with huge signs which read: STAY OUT, or CLOSED SET —THIS MEANS YOU. My own stage crew, not to be outdone, impishly put up a sign on our set which said: EVERY-BODY WELCOME BUT FRANKENHEIMER. STAY OUT—YOU.

If there are any conclusions to be drawn from this episode —and in the telling, it now seems foolish and childish to me— it is that Linkletter is not always a grinning clown who is too busy with horseplay to fight for his rights. I lose patience with performers who nurse the notion that talent automatically gives them the privilege of imposing their so-called artistic temperament on little people who can't fight back without risking their jobs. There are many kind, generous stars in the industry and their good work can be undone by one individual who consistently can't control either his temper or his tongue.

In any case, I am certain that the people in the studio audience that day, to say nothing of the millions watching us on their home screens, were astounded when Linkletter, who loves everybody, suddenly turned tiger.

v

It seems to me that I am almost always out in the evening— dinner parties, benefits, screenings, business meetings and other affairs—but once in a while I become the average man and settle down in a chair in front of the television set.

On those occasions, of course, I am subjected to movies that are old enough to earn Social Security, but even the ancient films have that magic touch which has made the motion picture one of the miracles of our time. I get particular delight from the slapstick nonsense of Laurel and Hardy, Abbott and Costello and the Three Stooges, and I am easily fractured when one of them skids on a banana, gets a pie in the face, or falls off a ladder. My reaction seems logical, considering that I spent years inventing similar stunts for People Are Funny.

But it is ironic that I cringe at the thought of being involved in these gags myself.

I cannot seem to make it clear, when this subject invariably comes up, that the contestants on the People Are Funny show are not only volunteers, but that they are being substantially rewarded for making idiots of themselves.

Nevertheless, in Hollywood there is a continuing conspiracy to determine if I can take it the way I dish it out. I not only can take it, but for professional reasons I am forced to laugh at myself.

I can never get into a bathtub without remembering a trip to Denver some years ago. Dick Pettit and some other members of my staff were usually late sleepers, and perhaps it bothered them a little when I would leap out of bed, jump into the tub shower and burst into song.

So one evening after I had gone to bed, they sneaked into my bathroom with a case of Jello—all six flavors of it—and stirred it into a tub of warm water. They drew the shower curtain and went out giggling. The next morning I bounded into the bathroom, flipped on the cold water faucet, yanked the curtain and stepped into a foot of goo. Pettit claims he found me knee deep in this slithery bog, laughing hysterically, but I doubt it. The bathtub Jello gag is one of history's oldest, and I not only objected to the mess, but I was disappointed that they had not thought of something more original.

I was on the famed Rancheros Ride in Santa Barbara County one year—this is an annual California event in which some four hundred tired businessmen ride horseback in the hills for seven days—and I had retired early. Along toward midnight I dreamed I was drowning—and I was. The jokers had run a hose into my sleeping bag, and it took some frantic backstroking to get me out of there. I was standing outside my tent, dripping, shivering and burning up, when from the bushes came the taunting cry: "Pee-pul are fun-n-n-y!" Did I laugh? I'll say I did. In a snarling sort of way.

Another year on the same ride, the comics in my tent sent for a sanitarium ambulance one midnight and told the white-coated orderlies: "One of our men has gone berserk and imagines he's Art Linkletter." My pals wrestled me to the ground, and I was put in a real strait jacket. I was halfway down the mountain, struggling to get free before I could convince the ambulance men it was just a joke. They didn't think it was funny at all—neither did I—and it took some shame-faced apologies to stall off a suit by the hospital.

Another time, I got into a crowded elevator with Jack Dempsey, and he used me for a trick that must have been gray and whiskered when he fought Carpentier back in the Twenties. As the cage started down, Jack reached around in front of me and delicately pinched a woman where she had probably not been pinched for some time.

She turned in fury just as Dempsey said loudly: "Up to your old stunts, eh, Art?" The woman belted me with her handbag and Dempsey went into hysterics. I haven't seen Dempsey since, and perhaps that's just as well.

Even around the house, especially when there are guests, the feeling persists that at any moment someone will toss a firecracker into the fireplace, or hide a small horse in the guest room. I am unable to convince most visitors that such shenanigans are confined to the studio. Air Force General Ira C. Eaker and his wife came to the house for dinner one evening, and somehow Mrs. Eaker imprisoned herself in an upstairs bathroom. When we finally got her out by forcing the lock, I went downstairs and found General Eaker, who hadn't budged during all the excitement, still calmly playing bridge.

"You don't seem to realize, General," I said, "that your wife might have been locked up there all night."

"Now, Art," he said quietly, dealing out a new hand, "you know this was just one of your little jokes."

16. American Grandstand

> *We were sitting around the breakfast table at home one morning when my son Jack, who was then about thirteen, looked up from his corn flakes and gave me a searching look.*
>
> *"Dad . . ." he said, "is it true that Mom's going to have another baby?"*
>
> *I choked on my scrambled eggs for a moment and finally found my tongue. "It's true, Jack," I said, "but who told you? I haven't breathed a word about it to anybody."*
>
> *"Yeah?" he said. "Well, I just read about it in Variety."*

THERE IS NOTHING SACRED, private or secret in Hollywood. At least, not in my business.

We are as exposed as the fish in the big tank at Marineland. When we go out to dinner at some public dining spot, the restaurant press agent jots it down in his little book. At the airport, boarding a plane, the airline flack reports our departure. At the office my own press agent hovers in the background with his ears working like radar and records any little item he thinks he can use. There are girls opening my mail. There are girls taking my phone calls. If I stay up late at a neighbor's party or dent the fender on my car or pull a boner on my shows, you can be positive that Louella and Hedda will hear about it. And if *Variety* says Lois is going to have a baby— though this might even be news to me—you know they've tapped the grapevine that leads directly to the doctor's confidential file.

I have heard many a star bitterly maintain that if he wants to mangle his wife or push his agent off a cliff it is his personal and private business, and not for public consumption.

The fact is—and I have long since accepted it as inevitable— that a man who comes into your living room via television once or twice or even five times a week seems no less a member of the family than the kid brother or the crotchety old uncle, and he is treated accordingly. When people are no longer curious about a performer's private life, you can be certain that his rating has dropped and he may have to go back to shoe-shining or modeling or burglary or whatever he did before he became a star.

There are certain drawbacks to the fishbowl life, and at times my patience and good nature do not quite survive the test.

The impending birth of another small Linkletter as exclusively forecast by *Variety*, for instance, precipitated one of those discordant episodes I would rather have done without. Shortly after Lois had reserved a hospital room for the birth of the little girl we named Sharon, I had a phone call from a network press agent who seemed more nervous about the coming event than either of us.

"Art," he said, "wouldn't it be possible for Lois to have a Caesarian?"

"It would be possible," I said, "but luckily she's never had any such problems. Why do you ask?"

"Well . . . ," he said, "I've been thinking that if Lois had a Caesarian . . . say, about nine o'clock at night . . . we would make the home editions of the morning papers with the story."

My reaction to this idea almost burned the insulation out of the phone wires, of course. But after I cooled down I realized that most press agents, in the mortal struggle to get valuable newspaper space for their stars or shows or networks and thus hold their jobs, occasionally reach into outer space for such wild ideas.

Actually, with certain reservations, I am happy if my friends and fans are interested in what the Linkletters do.

It is certainly no secret that we live in a roomy brick house—it's really a dormitory—on South Mapleton Drive in the Holmby Hills area of West Los Angeles. The tourist buses roll up and down the street almost every day, and we have been around that neighborhood long enough to have the house marked on the "Homes of the Stars" maps you can buy anywhere in Hollywood.

(In case there are Hollywood researchers, columnists, gossip gatherers, scandal magazine spies or others who don't get into our neighborhood often enough, I thought it would simplify their jobs if I did a sort of Inside Linkletter report myself.)

The other afternoon I was sitting at home, daydreaming about beautiful women, capital gains, roast beef and all the other ingredients of the good life, and I happened to look out the window and see the thing.

It was an old truck, noisily gear-grinding its way along our block, and fastened to it was an enormous sign about fifteen feet long, with crude hand-lettered words which read: LINK-LETTER IS NO GOOD. At first I thought it was a gag, dreamed up by some of the fun-loving friends who delight in ribbing me. But when the truck turned around, showing a sign on the other side which read LINKLETTER IS A JERK, I began to feel uneasy.

For the next ten minutes, the driver went up and down the

street, and with every trip my blood pressure went up. Perhaps I was a no-good jerk to him but I didn't want him to advertise it. I finally phoned the police, and a couple of gendarmes in a squad car stopped the truck and asked the driver, a bleary-eyed unshaven man, what the hell was the idea. It turned out he was a psycho who, though I had never seen him before, imagined that I had plotted to get him fired from one job after another. There was no prosecution, of course, and the unfortunate man was taken to a Los Angeles mental hospital for treatment.

I suppose I should have anticipated, when we moved into the Holmby Hills district, that we would not be living on some remote island.

Most neighborhoods reflect the personalities of the residents, and since our section of Los Angeles is studded with the homes of people who have unusual creative talent, it was certain to be more exciting than a subdivision in the Mojave Desert. When we moved to Mapleton Drive ten years ago, the first house on our block was occupied by Miss Lana Turner. Judy Garland soon moved next door to her and across the street from us was one of the great actors of our times, the late Humphrey Bogart, and his wife, the sultry and sexy Lauren Bacall.

On one side of our fence, in a charming house, is songwriter Sammy Cahn, and our youngsters have learned they can get private auditions of prize-winning melodies long before Tin Pan Alley gets around to putting them out.

Within a radius of a few blocks were the homes of Alan and Sue Ladd, Sonja Henie, Jane Wyman, Walter Wanger and his wife, Joan Bennett, composer Hoagy Carmichael and Bing Crosby. If your maid knew any of the other maids and cooks on the block, you could get along without Hedda and Winchell. Indeed, you got spicy information few columnists would have the nerve to print.

If we ran out of gossip about the stars, we could always talk about what we call the "mystery house." This house, on a small estate next door to us, was and is the only residence in the neighborhood for rent, furnished. The rent, or so the snoopers say, is fifteen hundred a month. Broadway producer Josh Logan was there for a while, so was Curt Jurgens, the suave Continental actor. Then came lover Porfirio Rubirosa, who had just walked out on his bride, Barbara Hutton. And whenever perky little Zsa Zsa Gabor spun down the street to call on him there were nosy observers peeking out their windows.

After Rubirosa came one of the young sons of General Trujillo, the Dominican Republic dictator, and sinister-looking bodyguards patrolled outside or kept themselves busy stacking empty champagne bottles in the back yard. Jayne Mansfield fluttered through that house on an inspection tour a couple of times but, alas, finally picked another mansion two blocks away. There she has a heart-shaped swimming pool, and we hear that low-flying airplane pilots looking for landmarks often lose altitude and direction when they dip down over Jayne's yard and see her paddling around.

As time passed, we not only met all our neighbors but became their friends and fellow conspirators. There was one period when Humphrey Bogart, who had come down out of the hills to live on Mapleton Drive, had three very noisy boxer dogs. These creatures became pugnacious in their new city surroundings and barked at every passing car day and night. Insomnia became a neighborhood disease, and there were frazzled nerves in every house. We asked Bogart to lock up his beasts at night, but he told us . . . well, I've forgotten exactly what he said, but it was unmistakably pure Bogart.

Eventually some of us had a meeting at the home of Charlie Correll, who is the Andy of the Amos and Andy team. Among others present were Cy Howard, author of the "My Friend

Irma" television series, and Welton Becket, the noted architect, whose small cocker spaniel had aged ten years since the boxers moved in. We decided to call the police, and presently a plain-clothes cop showed up and made notes as the bleary-eyed committee explained the problem.

"Well, ladies and gentlemen," the officer said with a faint smile, "there's no doubt that Mr. Bogart's dogs are a nuisance, and you have a legitimate complaint. But I should advise you that you'll all have to go to court, and the newspapers will probably be there. Maybe you ought to think it over."

We looked at one another sheepishly, and had a brief huddle. We thought about the court and the newspapers and about how tough Mr. Bogart could be, and decided the heck with it. The dogs kept right on barking, and we kept on losing sleep. The truth is—I liked Bogie with or without dogs. I admired his personal courage, and the movies suffered an irreplaceable loss when he died.

ii

My day begins when I am awakened by a musical alarm clock.

I need eight hours of sleep to get my metabolism going after what has usually been a fully packed sixteen-hour day, and I loll around until eight o'clock or so, but this is purely a personal indulgence. When I was ten or twelve years old and working a newspaper delivery route in San Diego, I had to get up in the dark, and it always aggravated me a little to throw the papers toward houses where the occupants were blissfully snoozing away.

Some of my friends in show business get the bends climbing out of bed at eight, and they need all sorts of booster shots to get going—black coffee, a thimble of vodka, a cold shower or an apprehensive glance at the stock market reports. I don't need anything—neither coffee nor orange juice nor a clock that goes off like an air raid siren—and I imagine that in Hollywood this makes me some sort of a freak.

At the breakfast table—it is no longer the noisy ritual it was when all five of our children were at home—I eat a rather light meal of fruit, eggs and toast. Often I am joined at breakfast by friends and business associates, all of whom are involved in a caloric war and who nevertheless gobble up enough hot cakes, sausages, syrup and butter to make their chairs creak. I am enormously amused by the fact that most of these gourmands, virtually gasping after a big meal, religiously drop a sucaryl tablet into their coffee and are thus cleansed of their gustatory sins.

It takes me eight minutes to drive from my home to my office on Beverly Boulevard, and our office girls could make book on my arrival and not be wrong by more than a few seconds or so.

The habits of a lifetime are as binding as handcuffs, and I find it impossible to avoid scheduling my time. I started disciplining myself to squeeze the most from every minute and hour when I was in school, and this attitude of mine disconcerts people who don't know that I am a slave to the clock. I remember a brash young insurance man in Los Angeles who phoned one busy day and said: "Art, I want to talk to you about insurance—and don't say no. I will need just one minute of your time. Just one minute."

"If that's the way you want it," I said, "okay."

He came to my office, sat down and started to talk. I had a stop watch in my hand, and he was still rambling on about the smog and the Dodgers and Marilyn Monroe when his sixty seconds were up. "That's it," I said. " 'Bye."

He was incredulous. "You're kidding, Art," he said.

"Didn't you ask for one minute?" I said.

"Yes," he admitted.

I got up and showed him out. I am sure he is roaming around Los Angeles telling people I am an oddball, but this is one of the risks I accept because I have only one short life to live, and I don't want to waste one precious minute.

This devotion to schedule is one of the less lovable things about me, I suppose, but it is an addiction I am unable to cure.

Lois and I, for instance, often go out with a certain star who must be nameless because he has a big television show and might tell lies about me. When we get to his house, en route to a party somewhere, I am nettled to find him still in his robe, putting the last dozen licks on his hair and gulping down the vitamin pills that will get him through the evening. I poke my head into his bathroom door and yell: "Hurry up, we're three minutes late!" He ignores me, and I fret and fume and swear I'll never go out with him again. But I do.

The Linkletters are notorious in Hollywood for arriving at parties exactly on time and finding their hostess still taking the curlers out of her hair. I am almost driven to homicide by people who invite us for seven when they mean eight, and there have been occasions when, with both of us looking pretty foolish, Lois and I have sat around living rooms for thirty or forty minutes until the next guests arrived.

Timetable living is fine for railroad people and the Linkletters, but unfortunately not everyone has confidence in regularity. One October evening, Lois and I went to Chasen's in Beverly Hills for dinner, and we were greeted there by our old friend Dave Chasen.

"Hello, Art," he said. "Doing a show somewhere tonight?"

"Not exactly a show," I said. "We're on our way to the hospital, and we'll have to have dinner in a hurry."

"Somebody sick? Anybody I know?"

"No. Lois is having a baby tonight."

"W-h-a-a-t?" he stammered.

"Now don't get excited," I said. "The pains are only two or three minutes apart now, and it'll be another hour before they get down to a minute. I'll keep my stop watch on the table, and you just go ahead and get us served."

Chasen's face was suddenly chalky, and I doubt if there has ever been more panic and confusion in that kitchen. Waiters came in relays, and the chefs, white caps askew, were all thumbs as they threw things together. The excitement around the restaurant reminded me of a zany stunt we had used during the early years of the People Are Funny show, when a contestant would ring the doorbell at some home and shout at the housewife: "Hurry—get towels and hot water ready! I've got a woman with a stork in the car and there's no time to lose!" The housewife would dash around like crazy and would come running out to the sidewalk with towels and sponges and a bucket of steaming water. And there she would find a woman and a stork we had borrowed from the zoo.

And that's how it was at Chasen's. There were no obstetricians on the staff and they wanted us out of there. Lois and I just sat serenely in our booth timing the pains as Chasen perspired, and we reached the hospital at exactly the right moment. We had a little girl, and we kiddingly toyed with the idea of calling her Chasen Linkletter. But she was so tiny and ethereal and had such enormous round eyes that we named her Diane after the goddess who, in mythology, is identified with the moon. I took her to meet Dave Chasen not long ago and he said, gallantly: "You almost gave me a nervous breakdown the night you were born, but if I'd known you were going to be so pretty I might have stalled the chefs long enough to have you delivered right here."

iii

The sun was bright and warm along the ocean highway one day about a year ago and, as happy couples will, Lois and I were chatting about our home, our children and grand-children, and all the other cherished treasures that have come to me in twenty-five years of radio and television work.

Somewhere along the route I had switched on the car radio, and we were just half-listening to a newscast.

Suddenly I heard my name. The announcer was excitedly saying that Art Linkletter had probably been drowned in the crash of a Navy helicopter, and he promised the grim details as soon as reporters could get them.

I looked at Lois wide-eyed. Lois looked at me, and she could see that I was sitting there in reasonably good health. I drove on until we found a pay phone, called the radio station and asked them to announce that I was very much alive. I wanted this news broadcast at once, not only to reassure anyone in the family who might have heard the rumor, but also so that my competitors and certain critics would not waste their money celebrating my demise.

The facts were that earlier in the day I had climbed into the helicopter for the finale of my House Party show, which was being televised from an aircraft carrier off San Diego. There had been several helicopter accidents in the area, and the Navy had insisted that I wear a crash helmet and a Mae West. Just as our program time ran out, the helicopter took a sudden wild plunge toward the sea, and the television camera fade-out showed the aircraft seemingly plummeting to disaster. It was a close call at that, because the crewmen had forgotten to undo one of the helicopter's tie-down bands, but fortunately I was with a skilled pilot and he steadied the reeling craft. The TV audience was not told the outcome, however, and soon the rumor-spreaders had me ready for the undertaker.

The false report of my death gave me pause for thought, and I recalled the old popular belief that a drowning man sees his whole life passing in review just before he goes down for the third time. I began to wonder what I would see if my life were to unreel itself like that, and I comforted myself with the thought that this mental flashback would take so long that someone would surely save me. There has been so much. The blue days and the gay days. The magic and misery of show business. The screwballs and the brains. Great men and small. Good men and bad. Wonderful people everywhere.

I have never had much of a reputation as a philosopher, but I am tempted to agree with Carl Sandburg when he says: "I tell you the past is a bucket of ashes." But if I stir up this heap a little, and add a coal or two and fan it with some current thought, I may get the happy blend of past and present which mirrors my life today.

I have resolved, for instance, to adjust myself to the incontrovertible fact that I am now forty-eight years old and that this calls for some altered perspectives. When beautiful young girls in their twenties address me as "Sir," and when other bewitching maidens bow politely and say: "Hello, Mr. Linkletter, I went to school with your daughter, Dawn," I am jolted by that sobering denouement which comes to every man as he starts down the mountain he had climbed so desperately.

There was also a period when I played handball as often as three times a week, and it seems only yesterday that I was a better-than-average contestant in the national championships. Some weeks ago, one of my former competitors in this strenuous game—he was about my age—was playing at a certain gymnasium where there are always players waiting in line for a vacant court. My ill-fated friend took one swing at the ball and dropped dead, and the impatient athletes standing by stopped just long enough to carry him out and then jostled one another for the unexpected vacancy.

"I suppose you heard about your friend at the handball court," Lois said.

"Yes," I said. "Tough luck."

"Does it give you an idea?"

"It does, indeed," I said. "As of now, I'm only going to play twice a week."

I have further resolved to count to ten before I make public remarks that may be misunderstood (although then I will probably say them anyway). At one point during the recent splash in the press about integration, I said: "There's no such problem in my business. Color television, for instance, is the great leveler. No matter what color you are, you come out purple, with green lips." Another time, when I was making a speech in San Francisco, I made some references to the payola scandals and said: "I have never been on a fixed show, but I have been on some that needed repairs." Both these observations were thoroughly innocent, but the letter writers and the phone callers came up with all sorts of hidden meanings.

I may have made an even greater blunder when I was invited to a sumptuous dinner at the Santa Monica home of Maury Machris, the prominent Southern California oil man. At the dinner table I found myself seated in a group that included former President Harry S. Truman, Mrs. Truman, Ed Pauley, the wealthy and influential Democratic Party leader, and others.

The conversation naturally turned to politics—an explosive subject I generally avoid—and someone mentioned the name of Senator William Knowland.

"I never thought very much of some of the things he did as

a Senator," President Truman said, "but personally I liked and admired him very much."

"That's a coincidence, Mr. President," I kidded, "because that's how I've always felt about you."

Half the people at the table suddenly stiffened, as though they'd been dropped into a glacier, and there was a dreadful moment of silence during which I got some glances which in effect said: *Drop dead*. But the Trumans burst into laughter, and Linkletter was saved.

It later became my privilege to join other friends and associates in persuading President Truman to write his book *Mr. Citizen*, and I note it has been on the bestseller list for months. President Truman also taught me his trick method for avoiding finger fatigue from a line of ardent hand shakers. He said he grabs the other person's hand about halfway down the finger-tips, a grip that prevents any bone-crushing response. I use the full palm-to-palm grip myself because my fingers are still strong after all those years of handball, but one day I may have to switch to the Truman system.

There may be other resolutions I should make, and there are probably mistakes and personal faults I have left off my confessions list. But this I know: Over the years I have tried to project an image of a happy man dedicated to fun and laughter. The tragedians also have their contribution to make, but that role is not for me. If I kid other people about their foibles, I am just as ready to joke about my own. My hope is that tomorrow may be as gay and rich for everyone as it has been for me for so many years. The world needs laughter, and I intend to spread it around.

Echo: I Confess

THIS HAS BEEN my story—the confessions of a happy man.

The lexicographers may quarrel with me on this phrase, since to confess generally suggests an admission of sins—a crime or a fault or something private and hidden that a man mentions with reluctance or shame. But to confess also means an acknowledgment, or an avowal of faith, and this has been my theme. I confess that I am a happy man.

Du Maurier once said that "Happiness is like time and space; we make it and measure it ourselves. It is as fancy, as big, as little as you please."

I do not think that happiness is a clever television script, or a five thousand dollar check or a top-ranking show. It is not the vanquishing of a rival, nor your name in a column, nor a house with a pool.

To me, happiness is like a play that has lightness and darkness, motion and sound—and a heart. It is a baby's plaintive cry at night, and I have heard it often. It is the laughter of a child discovering the good things in the world, and I am blessed with such laughter every day of my life. It is the gentle, reassuring touch of Lois's hand when trouble darkens our days. It is the sensitive, appealing letter from a foster child in some distant land—and I have four such wards—telling us what keeps him going, the knowledge that he is loved and needed by someone.

Happiness to me is the weakness to say "yes" when my

logical mind says "no." It is a word of praise for work well done, or an enriching hour with a friend, time gained in the race of life. It is a family like mine—together on a camping trip high in the mountains, or at a picnic at the beach, or on an evening in October when, still incurably small boy, I go out with my youngsters and join them in "trick or treat." Anatole France once spoke about the domestic hearth and said of it: *"There* is the only real happiness." This has been the lesson of my life. Our family is a unit in an adventure of living, and an experiment in love. It has never failed.

I have no patent or copyright on these thoughts.

They are as old as the world itself. They are as new as the sunrise. They belong to people everywhere. Especially you.